D1314371

1st EDITION

Perspectives on Diseases and Disorders

Dementia

Sylvia Engdahl
Book Editor

PERSPECTIVES
On Diseases & Disorders

361.1219
PER

GALE
CENGAGE Learning

Detroit • New York • San Francisco • New Haven, Conn • Waterville, Maine • London

LIBRARY
Southern Union State Community College (WD)
Wadley, Alabama 36276

Elizabeth Des Chenes, *Director, Publishing Solutions*

© 2013 Greenhaven Press, a part of Gale, Cengage Learning

Gale and Greenhaven Press are registered trademarks used herein under license.

For more information, contact:
Greenhaven Press
27500 Drake Rd.
Farmington Hills, MI 48331-3535
Or you can visit our Internet site at gale.cengage.com

ALL RIGHTS RESERVED.
No part of this work covered by the copyright herein may be reproduced, transmitted, stored, or used in any form or by any means graphic, electronic, or mechanical, including but not limited to photocopying, recording, scanning, digitizing, taping, Web distribution, information networks, or information storage and retrieval systems, except as permitted under Section 107 or 108 of the 1976 United States Copyright Act, without the prior written permission of the publisher.

For product information and technology assistance, contact us at

Gale Customer Support, 1-800-877-4253
For permission to use material from this text or product, submit all requests online at www.cengage.com/permissions

Further permissions questions can be e-mailed to permissionrequest@cengage.com

Articles in Greenhaven Press anthologies are often edited for length to meet page requirements. In addition, original titles of these works are changed to clearly present the main thesis and to explicitly indicate the author's opinion. Every effort is made to ensure that Greenhaven Press accurately reflects the original intent of the authors. Every effort has been made to trace the owners of copyrighted material.

Cover image © Lightspring/Shutterstock.com.

LIBRARY OF CONGRESS CATALOGING-IN-PUBLICATION DATA

Dementia / Sylvia Engdahl, book editor.
     pages cm. -- (Perspectives on diseases and disorders)
   Summary: "Perspectives on Diseases and Disorders: Dementia: Each volume in this timely series provides essential information on a disease or disorder (symptoms, causes, treatments, cures, etc.); presents the controversies surrounding causes, alternative treatments, and other issues"-- Provided by publisher.
   Includes bibliographical references and index.
   ISBN 978-0-7377-6352-2 (hardback)
   1. Dementia--Popular works. I. Engdahl, Sylvia, editor of compilation.
   RC521.D4525 2013
   616.8'3--dc23
                                                                    2012041154

Printed in the United States of America
1 2 3 4 5 6 7 17 16 15 14 13

CONTENTS

   Lou Cannon

   Four years after leaving office, President Ronald
   Reagan became forgetful; in August 1994 he was
   diagnosed with early Alzheimer's disease. Knowing
   that his condition would get worse, he wrote a
   famous letter to the American public in the hope that
   his experience would raise awareness of the disease
   and understanding of the individuals and families
   affected by it.

FOREWORD

"Medicine, to produce health, has to examine disease."
—Plutarch

Independent research on a health issue is often the first step to complement discussions with a physician. But locating accurate, well-organized, understandable medical information can be a challenge. A simple Internet search on terms such as "cancer" or "diabetes," for example, returns an intimidating number of results. Sifting through the results can be daunting, particularly when some of the information is inconsistent or even contradictory. The Greenhaven Press series Perspectives on Diseases and Disorders offers a solution to the often overwhelming nature of researching diseases and disorders.

From the clinical to the personal, titles in the Perspectives on Diseases and Disorders series provide students and other researchers with authoritative, accessible information in unique anthologies that include basic information about the disease or disorder, controversial aspects of diagnosis and treatment, and first-person accounts of those impacted by the disease. The result is a well-rounded combination of primary and secondary sources that, together, provide the reader with a better understanding of the disease or disorder.

Each volume in Perspectives on Diseases and Disorders explores a particular disease or disorder in detail. Material for each volume is carefully selected from a wide range of sources, including encyclopedias, journals, newspapers, non-fiction books, speeches, government documents, pamphlets, organization newsletters, and position papers. Articles in the first chapter provide an authoritative, up-to-date overview that covers symptoms, causes and effects, treatments, cures, and medical advances. The second chapter presents a substantial number of opposing viewpoints on controversial treatments and other current debates relating to the volume topic. The third chapter offers a variety of personal perspectives on the disease or disorder. Patients, doctors, caregivers, and loved ones represent just some of the voices found in this narrative chapter.

Each Perspectives on Diseases and Disorders volume also includes:

- An **annotated table of contents** that provides a brief summary of each article in the volume.

- An **introduction** specific to the volume topic.

- Full-color **charts and graphs** to illustrate key points, concepts, and theories.

- Full-color **photos** that show aspects of the disease or disorder and enhance textual material.

- **"Fast Facts"** that highlight pertinent additional statistics and surprising points.

- A **glossary** providing users with definitions of important terms.

- A **chronology** of important dates relating to the disease or disorder.

- An annotated list of **organizations to contact** for students and other readers seeking additional information.

- A **bibliography** of additional books and periodicals for further research.

- A detailed **subject index** that allows readers to quickly find the information they need.

Whether a student researching a disorder, a patient recently diagnosed with a disease, or an individual who simply wants to learn more about a particular disease or disorder, a reader who turns to Perspectives on Diseases and Disorders will find a wealth of information in each volume that offers not only basic information, but also vigorous debate from multiple perspectives.

INTRODUCTION

Dementia is increasingly recognized as a major, and perhaps the greatest, public health problem of the twenty-first century. There is no known way to prevent it, no effective treatment, and no cure. It is devastating not only to its victims but to their families; those affected by it become completely dependent on others for round-the-clock care. They often live for years without memory of their earlier, active lives or even the ability to recognize loved ones. And the number of people with dementia is increasing rapidly. In 2010 there were over 35 million worldwide; it is expected that by 2050 there will be over 115 million.

The main reason for this rapid rise is that dementia is primarily a disease of old age, and people are living longer than they used to. Great progress is being made in preventing or curing diseases such as heart disease and cancer—but there is a downside to this progress. The people who once would have died from other diseases are now living long enough to get those that produce dementia. It strikes nearly half of those over age eighty-five. And so some older Americans are coming to view the lengthening of extreme old age as a mixed blessing, for dementia is something nobody wants to experience. "The phrase you often hear is that the 'Big A' (Alzheimer's) has replaced the 'Big C' (cancer) as a major source of fear," says Dr. Jason Karlawish, a University of Pennsylvania medical ethicist.

Although the primary risk factor for dementia is old age, it is not a normal part of aging. Until fairly recently, the forgetfulness and confusion of many old people was called "senility" and was commonly thought to be merely the result of being old. In reality, dementia is due to brain damage. It is not a disease in itself, but a symptom of various brain diseases that medical science does not yet understand. There are a number of different types of dementia, characterized by specific patterns of mental disability and specific abnormalities of the brain. However, except in the case of vascular dementia, scientists do not know what causes these abnormalities. And until they discover the cause, there is not much chance that they can find a means of prevention—let alone a cure, which would require reversing brain damage that has already occurred.

The search for the cause is not easy, as it requires studying individuals for many years, starting when they are young and even examining their brains after they die. Brain damage is not like a contagious disease with a rapid onset; it comes on very gradually over a long period. Until recently it could not be seen prior to autopsy, although brain scans can now detect some types while patients are alive. And there are so many variables in a person's life that even when data about past health is available, long-term comparative studies of groups are rarely feasible.

A few research studies have shed light on factors that may protect against dementia. One of them, called the Nun Study, investigates Catholic nuns who donated their brains when they died. Because nuns have very similar lives, with similar diets, routines, and occupations, it is possible to isolate specific ways in which they differ from each other. It has been found, for example, that those who have strong language skills when they are young get dementia in old age less often than others, even if they do have some brain damage. This is consistent with statistical studies showing that people who are well educated and read a lot, or who had mind-challenging hobbies in middle age, are also less apt to get dementia. Researchers think such people may have some sort of "brain reserve" that compensates for damage to some of their brain cells. But no one knows whether they had brain characteristics in the first place that led them to enjoy mental challenge, or if reading and hobbies caused them to develop this brain reserve.

Dementia is primarily a disease of old age, and its rapid rise is due to people living longer. (© **Paula Solloway/Alamy**)

In a small percentage of cases, certain genes predispose individuals to Alzheimer's disease. But the vast majority of cases are not of genetic origin. Many physical factors have been suggested as possible risk factors for dementia, and some authorities advise avoiding them throughout life as a preventative measure. However, in 2010 the report of an investigation by the National Institutes of Health stated: "Currently, no evidence of even moderate scientific quality exists to support the association of any modifiable factor (such as nutritional supplements, herbal preparations, dietary factors, prescription or nonprescription drugs, social or economic factors, medical conditions, toxins, or environmental exposures) with reduced risk of Alzheimer's disease." This is the case with most types of dementia; if a means of reducing risk does exist, it is something that has not yet been identified. Vascular dementia is an exception because it is caused by strokes or by the narrowing of blood vessel to the brain, and so practices that reduce risk for stroke and heart disease apply to it.

There are drugs that can help with some of the symptoms of dementia, and even a few that can slow its progress slightly in some people for a short time. Whether they offer significant benefits is debatable. Researchers are trying desperately to develop better drugs, but since they are not sure whether these treat the underlying cause of the brain damage, it is uncertain how long this will take.

High priority is being given to research on dementia. The US government is creating a national plan with the hope of finding effective treatments by 2025. This is of vital importance not only because of the suffering of dementia patients and their caregivers, but because the rising cost of long-term care puts a growing burden on society. Most patients are cared for in their homes by relatives, but those too sick for home care, or who have no relatives able to take them in, must go to nursing homes. Nursing home care for a person with dementia costs around eighty thousand to ninety thousand dollars per year in 2012, and few people are able to afford these payments for very long. When their money runs out, Medicaid, the government health-care program for the poor, has to pay, since Medicare, the program for the elderly, does not cover long-term care. In 2012 Medicaid paid over $35 billion toward the cost of caring for Alzheimer's patients. The total cost, including what people pay out of pocket and what Medicare pays for medical treatment, is expected to rise from $200 billion in 2012 to over $1 trillion in 2050. Economists are worried; they do not see where that much money is going to come from.

In one area there has been considerable progress toward understanding dementia: New knowledge has made it possible to diagnose dementia before it becomes disabling. It is important to diagnose the specific disease a dementia patient has, because different types require different drugs to help with symptoms; some of these drugs can be harmful for patients with a different disease. Moreover, caregivers need to know what to expect, as the course of disease progression for the different types is not the same.

The desirability of diagnosis in cases with minor symptoms—or even no symptoms at all—is controversial. Many doctors and other authorities believe that the earlier the diagnosis, the better, and that there should be a campaign to increase public awareness of warning signs and urge people to seek treatment. These authorities feel it is a good thing that forthcoming tests of biomarkers may be able to detect developing dementia before symptoms appear. Others, however, see no good reason for people to be told any sooner than it becomes evident to them that they are likely to get an incurable, progressive disease that will rob them of their minds, considering that there is no way to prevent dementia and no effective treatment if it develops—and that they might die of something else before that happens. There are individuals who want to be informed so they can plan ahead for care, or who want to try available treatments on the chance that they will help. On the other hand, many feel that this chance is too small to be worth spoiling the remainder of their good years with the knowledge of what lies ahead of them.

From the research standpoint, early diagnosis is essential so that the mechanism of disease progression can be studied and new drugs that might slow it can be tested. Nevertheless, whether to participate in research is an individual decision, and finding out that one has dementia before it has begun to seriously affect daily living is not necessarily the right course for everyone. Once an effective treatment is discovered, this will change; and hopefully that time will come soon.

CHAPTER 1

Understanding Dementia

An Overview of Dementia

National Institute of Neurological Disorders and Stroke

This article from the National Institute of Neurological Disorders and Stroke (NINDS) explains that many diseases of the brain produce dementia, which is the name given to a collection of symptoms involving cognitive impairment—that is, the loss of memory and of the ability to think clearly. The most common ones are Alzheimer's disease, vascular dementia, Lewy body dementia, and frontotemporal dementia. The specific brain defects and pattern of symptoms characteristic of these diseases are distinct, but they are all similar, and all are progressive and incurable. Scientists do not know what causes them. People with moderate or advanced dementia generally need round-the-clock supervision and assistance with the essential activities of daily life.

The NINDS is part the National Institutes of Health, an agency of the US government.

SOURCE: "Dementia: Hope Through Research," Office of Communications and Public Liaison, National Institute of Neurological Disorders and Stroke. National Institutes of Health, December 28, 2011.

Photo on facing page. German psychiatrist Alois Alzheimer first identified the illness that bears his name. (© Apic/Getty Images)

A woman in her early 50s was admitted to a hospital because of increasingly odd behavior. Her family reported that she had been showing memory problems and strong feelings of jealousy. She also had become disoriented at home and was hiding objects. During a doctor's examination, the woman was unable to remember her husband's name, the year, or how long she had been at the hospital. She could read but did not seem to understand what she read, and she stressed the words in an unusual way. She sometimes became agitated and seemed to have hallucinations and irrational fears.

This woman, known as Auguste D., was the first person reported to have the disease now known as *Alzheimer's disease* (AD) after Alois Alzheimer, the German doctor who first described it. After Auguste D. died in 1906, doctors examined her brain and found that it appeared shrunken and contained several unusual features, including strange clumps of protein called *plaques* and tangled fibers inside the nerve cells. Memory impairments and other symptoms of *dementia*, which means "deprived of mind," had been described in older adults since ancient times. However, because Auguste D. began to show symptoms at a relatively early age, doctors did not think her disease could be related to what was then called "*senile dementia*." The word senile is derived from a Latin term that means, roughly, "old age."

It is now clear that AD is a major cause of dementia in elderly people as well as in relatively young adults. Furthermore, we know that it is only one of many disorders that can lead to dementia. The U.S. Congress Office of Technology Assessment estimates that as many as 6.8 million people in the United States have dementia, and at least 1.8 million of those are severely affected. Studies in some communities have found that almost half of all people age 85 and older have some form of dementia. Although it is common in very elderly individuals, dementia is not a normal part of the aging process. Many people live into their 90s and even 100s without any symptoms of dementia.

Besides senile dementia, other terms often used to describe dementia include senility and *organic brain syndrome*. Senility and senile dementia are outdated terms that reflect the formerly widespread belief that dementia was a normal part of aging. Organic brain syndrome is a general term that refers to physical disorders (not psychiatric in origin) that impair mental functions.

Research in the last 30 years has led to a greatly improved understanding of what dementia is, who gets it, and how it develops and affects the brain. This work is beginning to pay off with better diagnostic techniques, improved treatments, and even potential ways of preventing these diseases.

What Is Dementia?

Dementia is not a specific disease. It is a descriptive term for a collection of symptoms that can be caused by a number of disorders that affect the brain. People with dementia have significantly impaired intellectual functioning that interferes with normal activities and relationships. They also lose their ability to solve problems and maintain emotional control, and they may experience personality changes and behavioral problems such as agitation, delusions, and hallucinations. While memory loss is a common symptom of dementia, memory loss by itself does not mean that a person has dementia. Doctors diagnose dementia only if two or more brain functions—such as memory, language skills, perception, or cognitive skills including reasoning and judgment—are significantly impaired without loss of consciousness.

There are many disorders that can cause dementia. Some, such as AD, lead to a progressive loss of mental functions. But other types of dementia can be halted or reversed with appropriate treatment.

With AD and many other types of dementia, disease processes cause many nerve cells to stop functioning, lose connections with other neurons, and die. In contrast, normal aging does not result in the loss of large numbers of neurons in the brain. . . .

Alzheimer's Disease

Alzheimer's disease is the most common cause of dementia in people aged 65 and older. Experts believe that up to 4 million people in the United States are currently living with the disease: one in ten people over the age of 65 and nearly half of those over 85 have AD. At least 360,000 Americans are diagnosed with AD each year and about 50,000 are reported to die from it.

In most people, symptoms of AD appear after age 60. However, there are some early-onset forms of the disease, usually linked to a specific gene defect, which may appear as early as age 30. AD usually causes a gradual decline in cognitive abilities, usually during a span of 7 to 10 years. Nearly all brain functions, including memory, movement, language, judgment, behavior, and abstract thinking, are eventually affected.

AD is characterized by two abnormalities in the brain: *amyloid plaques* and *neurofibrillary tangles*. Amyloid plaques, which are found in the tissue between the nerve cells, are unusual clumps of a protein called *beta amyloid* along with degenerating bits of neurons and other cells.

Neurofibrillary tangles are bundles of twisted filaments found within neurons. These tangles are largely made up of a protein called *tau*. In healthy neurons, the *tau* protein helps the functioning of microtubules, which are part of the cell's structural support and deliver substances throughout the nerve cell. However, in AD, *tau* is changed in a way that causes it to twist into pairs of helical filaments that collect into tangles. When this happens, the microtubules cannot function correctly and they disintegrate. This collapse of the neuron's transport system may impair communication between nerve cells and cause them to die.

Researchers do not know if amyloid plaques and neurofibrillary tangles are harmful or if they are merely side effects of the disease process that damages neurons and leads to the symptoms of AD. They do know that plaques and tangles usually increase in the brain as AD progresses.

In this illustration, plaques made up of amyloid proteins are shown developing around the neurons in the brain of an Alzheimer's patient. Researchers continue to investigate the role of plaques and neurofibrillary tangles in the development of Alzheimer's. (© Mark Phares/Photo Researchers, Inc.)

In the early stages of AD, patients may experience memory impairment, lapses of judgment, and subtle changes in personality. As the disorder progresses, memory and language problems worsen and patients begin to have difficulty performing activities of daily living, such as balancing a checkbook or remembering to take medications. They also may have visuospatial problems, such as difficulty navigating an unfamiliar route. They may become disoriented about places and times, may suffer delusions (such as the idea that someone is stealing from them or that their spouse is being unfaithful), and may become short-tempered and hostile. During the late stages of the disease, patients begin to lose the ability to control motor functions. They may have difficulty swallowing and lose bowel and bladder control. They eventually lose the ability to recognize family members and to speak. As AD progresses, it begins to affect the person's emotions and behavior. Most people with AD eventually develop symptoms such as aggression, agitation, depression, sleeplessness, or delusions.

On average, patients with AD live for 8 to 10 years after they are diagnosed. However, some people live as long as 20 years. Patients with AD often die of aspiration pneumonia because they lose the ability to swallow late in the course of the disease.

Vascular Dementia

Vascular dementia is the second most common cause of dementia, after AD. It accounts for up to 20 percent of all dementias and is caused by brain damage from cerebrovascular or cardiovascular problems—usually strokes. It also may result from genetic diseases, endocarditis (infection of a heart valve), or amyloid angiopathy (a process in which amyloid protein builds up in the brain's blood vessels, sometimes causing hemorrhagic or "bleeding" strokes). In many cases, it may coexist with AD. The incidence of vascular dementia increases with advancing age and is similar in men and women.

Symptoms of vascular dementia often begin suddenly, frequently after a stroke. Patients may have a history of high blood pressure, vascular disease, or previous strokes or heart attacks. Vascular dementia may or may not get worse with time, depending on whether the person has additional strokes. In some cases, symptoms may get better with time. When the disease does get worse, it often progresses in a stepwise manner, with sudden changes in ability. Vascular dementia with brain damage to the midbrain regions, however, may cause a gradual, progressive cognitive impairment that may look much like AD. Unlike people with AD, people with vascular dementia often maintain their personality and normal levels of emotional responsiveness until the later stages of the disease.

People with vascular dementia frequently wander at night and often have other problems commonly found in people who have had a stroke, including depression and incontinence.

There are several types of vascular dementia, which vary slightly in their causes and symptoms. One type, called *multi-infarct dementia (MID)*, is caused by numerous small strokes in the brain. MID typically includes multiple damaged areas, called infarcts, along with extensive lesions in the white matter, or nerve fibers, of the brain.

Because the infarcts in MID affect isolated areas of the brain, the symptoms are often limited to one side of the body or they may affect just one or a few specific functions, such as language. Neurologists call these "local" or "focal" symptoms, as opposed to the "global" symptoms seen in AD, which affect many functions and are not restricted to one side of the body.

Although not all strokes cause dementia, in some cases a single stroke can damage the brain enough to cause dementia. This condition is called single-infarct dementia. Dementia is more common when the stroke takes place on the left side (hemisphere) of the brain and/or when it involves the hippocampus, a brain structure important for memory. . . .

Lewy Body Dementia

Lewy body dementia (LBD) is one of the most common types of progressive dementia. LBD usually occurs sporadically, in people with no known family history of the disease. However, rare familial cases have occasionally been reported.

In LBD, cells die in the brain's cortex, or outer layer, and in a part of the mid-brain called the substantia nigra. Many of the remaining nerve cells in the substantia nigra contain abnormal structures called Lewy bodies that are the hallmark of the disease. Lewy bodies may also appear in the brain's cortex, or outer layer. . . .

The symptoms of LBD overlap with AD in many ways, and may include memory impairment, poor judgment, and confusion. However, LBD typically also includes visual hallucinations, parkinsonian symptoms [symptoms similar to those of Parkinson's disease] such as a shuffling gait and flexed posture, and day-to-day fluctuations in the severity of symptoms. Patients with LBD live an average of 7 years after symptoms begin.

There is no cure for LBD, and treatments are aimed at controlling the parkinsonian and psychiatric symptoms of the disorder. . . .

Lewy bodies are often found in the brains of people with Parkinson's and AD. These findings suggest that either LBD is related to these other causes of dementia or that the diseases sometimes coexist in the same person.

Frontotemporal Dementia

Frontotemporal dementia (FTD), sometimes called frontal lobe dementia, describes a group of diseases characterized by degeneration of nerve cells—especially those in the frontal and temporal lobes of the brain. Unlike AD, FTD usually does not include formation of amyloid plaques. In many people with FTD, there is an abnormal form of *tau* protein in the brain, which accumulates into neurofibrillary tangles. This disrupts normal cell activities and may cause the cells to die.

Experts believe FTD accounts for 2 to 10 percent of all cases of dementia. Symptoms of FTD usually appear between the ages of 40 and 65. In many cases, people with FTD have a family history of dementia, suggesting that there is a strong genetic factor in the disease. The duration of FTD varies, with some patients declining rapidly over 2 to 3 years and others showing only minimal changes for many years. People with FTD live with the disease for an average of 5 to 10 years after diagnosis.

Because structures found in the frontal and temporal lobes of the brain control judgment and social behavior, people with FTD often have problems maintaining normal interactions and following social conventions. They may steal or exhibit impolite and socially inappropriate behavior, and they may neglect their normal responsibilities. Other common symptoms include loss of speech and language, compulsive or repetitive behavior, increased appetite, and motor problems such as stiffness and balance problems. Memory loss also may occur, although it typically appears late in the disease.

> **FAST FACT**
>
> Mild cognitive impairment (MCI) is a condition in which a person has noticeable changes in thinking ability that are not serious enough to interfere with daily life. People who have MCI are more likely to develop dementia than those who do not.

In one type of FTD called *Pick's disease*, certain nerve cells become abnormal and swollen before they die. These swollen, or ballooned, neurons are one hallmark of the disease. The brains of people with Pick's disease also have abnormal structures called Pick bodies, composed largely of the protein *tau*, inside the neurons. The cause of Pick's disease is unknown, but it runs in some families and thus it is probably due at least in part to a faulty gene or genes. The disease usually begins after age 50 and causes changes in personality and behavior that gradually worsen over time. The symptoms of Pick's disease are very similar to those of AD, and may include inappropriate social behavior, loss of mental flexibility, language problems, and difficulty with thinking and concentration. There is currently no way to slow the progressive degeneration found in Pick's disease. However, medication may be helpful in reducing aggression and other behavioral problems, and in treating depression. . . .

What Causes Dementia?

All forms of dementia result from the death of nerve cells and/or the loss of communication among these cells. The human brain is a very complex and intricate machine and many factors can interfere with its functioning. Researchers have uncovered many of these factors, but they have not yet been able to fit these puzzle pieces together in order to form a complete picture of how dementias develop.

Many types of dementia, including AD, Lewy body dementia, Parkinson's dementia, and Pick's disease, are characterized by abnormal structures called inclusions in the brain. Because these inclusions, which contain abnormal proteins, are so common in people with dementia, researchers suspect that they play a role in the development of symptoms. However, that role is unknown, and in some cases the inclusions may simply be a side effect of the disease process that leads to the dementia.

Genes clearly play a role in the development of some kinds of dementia. However, in AD and many other disorders, the dementia usually cannot be tied to a single abnormal gene. Instead, these forms of dementia appear to result from a complex interaction of genes, lifestyle factors, and other environmental influences. . . .

Vascular dementia can be caused by cerebrovascular disease or any other condition that prevents normal blood flow to the brain. Without a normal supply of blood, brain cells cannot obtain the oxygen they need to work correctly, and they often become so deprived that they die. . . .

Is There Any Treatment?

While treatments to reverse or halt disease progression are not available for most of the dementias, patients can benefit to some extent from treatment with available medications and other measures, such as *cognitive training*.

Drugs to specifically treat AD and some other progressive dementias are now available and are prescribed for many patients. Although these drugs do not halt the disease or reverse existing brain damage, they can improve symptoms and slow the progression of the disease. This may improve the patient's quality of life, ease the burden on caregivers, and/or delay admission to a nursing home. Many researchers are also examining whether these drugs may be useful for treating other types of dementia.

Many people with dementia, particularly those in the early stages, may benefit from practicing tasks designed to improve performance in specific aspects of cognitive functioning. For example, people can sometimes be taught to use memory aids, such as mnemonics, computerized recall devices, or note taking.

Behavior modification—rewarding appropriate or positive behavior and ignoring inappropriate behavior—also may help control unacceptable or dangerous behaviors.

Research has revealed a number of factors that may be able to prevent or delay the onset of dementia in some people. For example, studies have shown that people who maintain tight control over their glucose levels tend to score better on tests of cognitive function than those with poorly controlled diabetes. Several studies also have suggested that people who engage in intellectually stimulating activities, such as social interactions, chess, crossword puzzles, and playing a musical instrument, significantly lower their risk of developing AD and other forms of dementia. Scientists believe mental activities may stimulate the brain in a way that increases the person's "cognitive reserve"—the ability to cope with or compensate for the pathologic changes associated with dementia.

Researchers are studying other steps people can take that may help prevent AD in some cases. So far, none of these factors has been definitively proven to make a difference in the risk of developing the disease. Moreover, most of the studies addressed only AD, and the results may or may not apply to other forms of dementia. Nevertheless, scientists are encouraged by the results of these early studies and many believe it will eventually become possible to prevent some forms of dementia. . . .

What Care Does a Person with Dementia Need?

People with moderate and advanced dementia typically need round-the-clock care and supervision to prevent them from harming themselves or others. They also may need assistance with daily activities such as eating, bathing, and dressing. Meeting these needs takes patience, understanding, and careful thought by the person's caregivers.

A typical home environment can present many dangers and obstacles to a person with dementia, but simple changes can overcome many of these problems. For example, sharp knives, dangerous chemicals, tools, and other hazards should be removed or locked away. Other safety measures include installing bed and bathroom safety rails, removing locks from bedroom and bathroom doors, and lowering the hot water temperature to 120°F (48.9°C) or less to reduce the risk of accidental scalding. People with dementia also should wear some form of identification at all times in case they wander away or become lost. Caregivers can help prevent unsupervised wandering by adding locks or alarms to outside doors.

People with dementia often develop behavior problems because of frustration with specific situations. Understanding and modifying or preventing the situations

The Main Types of Dementia

Type of Dementia	Description
Alzheimer's disease (AD)	Very common in old age; brain contains plaques and tangles
Vascular dementia (VaD)	Second most common; caused by impaired blood supply to brain
Lewy body dementia (LBD or DLB)	Fairly common; brain contains structures called Lewy bodies
Frontotemporal dementia (FTD)	Appears in middle age; Pick's disease is the most common form
Parkinson's disease dementia (PDD)	20–30 percent of people with Parkinson's disease; involves Lewy bodies
Huntington's disease (HD)	Hereditary; caused by a faulty gene
HIV-associated dementia (HAV)	Caused by the HIV virus that causes AIDS
Dementia pugilistica (boxer's syndrome)	Caused by repeated head trauma
Corticobasal degeneration (CBD)	Uncommon; characterized by atrophy of the brain
Creutzfeldt-Jakob disease (CJD)	Rare; one form caused by contamination with mad cow disease
Normal pressure hydrocephalus	Caused by buildup of fluid in the brain

Taken from: NINDS. "Dementia: Hope Through Research." December 28, 2011. www.ninds.nih.gov/disorders /dementias/details_dementia.htm#1909819213Introduction.

that trigger these behaviors may help to make life more pleasant for the person with dementia as well as his or her caregivers. For instance, the person may be confused or frustrated by the level of activity or noise in the surrounding environment. Reducing unnecessary activity and noise (such as limiting the number of visitors and turning off the television when it's not in use) may make it easier for the person to understand requests and perform simple tasks. Confusion also may be reduced by simplifying home decorations, removing clutter, keeping familiar objects nearby, and following a predictable routine throughout the day. Calendars and clocks also may help patients orient themselves.

People with dementia should be encouraged to continue their normal leisure activities as long as they are safe and do not cause frustration. Activities such as crafts, games, and music can provide important mental stimulation and improve mood. Some studies have suggested that participating in exercise and intellectually stimulating activities may slow the decline of cognitive function in some people.

Many studies have found that driving is unsafe for people with dementia. They often get lost and they may have problems remembering or following rules of the road. They also may have difficulty processing information quickly and dealing with unexpected circumstances. Even a second of confusion while driving can lead to an accident. Driving with impaired cognitive functions can also endanger others. Some experts have suggested that regular screening for changes in cognition might help to reduce the number of driving accidents among elderly people, and some states now require that doctors report people with AD to their state motor vehicle department. However, in many cases, it is up to the person's family and friends to ensure that the person does not drive.

The emotional and physical burden of caring for someone with dementia can be overwhelming. Support groups can often help caregivers deal with these demands and they can also offer helpful information about the disease and its treatment. It is important that caregivers occasionally have time off from round-the-clock nursing demands. Some communities provide respite facilities or adult day care centers that will care for dementia patients for a period of time, giving the primary caregivers a break. Eventually, many patients with dementia require the services of a full-time nursing home.

Ten Warning Signs of Alzheimer's Disease

Alzheimer's Association

The Alzheimer's Association, the leading nonprofit global health organization providing care, support, and research funding for Alzheimer's disease (AD), lists ten warning signs of AD that can help people distinguish between its early stages and normal aging. Forgetting or losing things temporarily or occasionally showing poor judgment is normal; but when such problems occur often and involve things familiar to a person or begin to affect daily life, that indicates possible dementia. The key is whether there is a significant change from the person's previous behavior.

I t may be hard to know the difference between a typical age-related change and the first sign of Alzheimer's disease. Ask yourself: Is this something new? For example, if the person was never good at balancing a checkbook, struggling with this task is probably not a warning sign. But if his or her ability

SOURCE: "Ten Warning Signs of Alzheimer's Disease," in *Basics of Alzheimer's Disease,* Alzheimer's Association, 2012. Copyright © 2012 Alzheimer's Association. All rights reserved. Used with permission.

One of the most common symptoms of Alzheimer's is forgetting recently learned information and important dates or events. To remember, patients often must rely on memory aids such as written notes. (© Olivier Volsin)

to balance a checkbook has significantly changed, it is something to share with a doctor.

Some people recognize changes in themselves before anyone else does. Other times, friends and family are the first to notice changes in the person's memory, behavior or abilities.

To help, the Alzheimer's Association has created a list of warning signs for Alzheimer's disease. Individuals may experience one or more of these in different degrees. If you notice any of them, please see a doctor.

1. Memory loss that disrupts daily life

One of the most common signs of Alzheimer's disease, especially in the early stages, is forgetting recently learned information. Others include forgetting important dates or events; asking for the same information over and over; and relying on memory aides (e.g., reminder notes or electronic devices) or family members for things they used to handle on their own.

What's a typical age-related change?

Sometimes forgetting names or appointments, but remembering them later.

2. Challenges in planning or solving problems

Some people may experience changes in their ability to develop and follow a plan or work with numbers. They may have trouble following a familiar recipe or keeping track of monthly bills. They may have difficulty concentrating and take much longer to do things than they did before.

What's a typical age-related change?

Making occasional errors when balancing a checkbook.

3. Difficulty completing familiar tasks at home, at work or at leisure

People with Alzheimer's disease often find it hard to complete daily tasks. Sometimes, people have trouble driving to a familiar location, managing a budget at work or remembering the rules of a favorite game.

What's a typical age-related change?

Occasionally needing help to use the settings on a microwave or to record a television show.

FAST FACT

According to the World Health Organization, the 35.6 million people with dementia make up 0.5 percent of the world's population—in other words, one out of two hundred people in the world is affected by it.

---

4. Confusion with time or place

People with Alzheimer's can lose track of dates, seasons and the passage of time. They may have trouble understanding something if it is not happening immediately. Sometimes they may forget where they are or how they got there.

What's a typical age-related change?

Getting confused about the day of the week but figuring it out later.

5. Trouble understanding visual images and spatial relationships

For some people, having vision problems is a sign of Alzheimer's. They may have difficulty reading, judging distance and determining color or contrast. In terms of perception, they may pass a mirror and think someone else is in the room. They may not realize they are the person in the mirror.

What's a typical age-related change?

Vision changes related to cataracts.

6. New problems with words in speaking or writing

People with Alzheimer's may have trouble following or joining a conversation. They may stop in the middle of a conversation and have no idea how to continue or they may repeat themselves. They may struggle with vocabulary, have problems finding the right word or call things by the wrong name (e.g., calling a watch a "hand clock").

What's a typical age-related change?

Sometimes having trouble finding the right word.

Annual Incidence of Dementia Throughout the World

This graph shows how many new cases of dementia there are each year among people in different age groups.

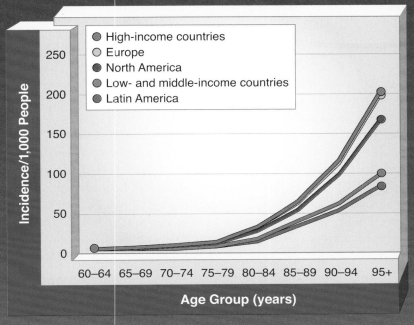

Taken from: World Health Organization, Dementia: A Public Health Priority, April 2012. http://whqlibdoc.who.int/publications/2012/9789241564458_eng.pdf.

7. Misplacing things and losing the ability to retrace steps

A person with Alzheimer's disease may put things in unusual places. They may lose things and be unable to go back over their steps to find them again. Sometimes, they may accuse others of stealing. This may occur more frequently over time.

What's a typical age-related change?

Misplacing things from time to time, such as a pair of glasses or the remote control.

8. Decreased or poor judgment

People with Alzheimer's may experience changes in judgment or decision making. For example, they may use poor judgment when dealing with money, giving large amounts to telemarketers. They may pay less attention to grooming or keeping themselves clean.

What's a typical age-related change?

Making a bad decision once in a while.

9. Withdrawal from work or social activities

A person with Alzheimer's may start to remove themselves from hobbies, social activities, work projects or sports. They may have trouble keeping up with a favorite sports team or remembering how to complete a favorite hobby. They may also avoid being social because of the changes they have experienced.

What's a typical age-related change?

Sometimes feeling weary of work, family and social obligations.

10. Changes in mood and personality

The mood and personality of people with Alzheimer's can change. They can become confused, suspicious, depressed, fearful or anxious. They may be easily upset at home, at work, with friends or in places where they are out of their comfort zone.

What's a typical age-related change?

Developing very specific ways of doing things and becoming irritable when a routine is disrupted.

Note: Mood changes with age may also be a sign of some other condition. Consult a doctor if you observe any changes.

Vascular Dementia Is Caused by Impaired Blood Flow to the Brain

Carrie Hill

Impaired blood flow to the brain can result in a type of dementia known as vascular dementia. It used to be called multi-infarct dementia because it was thought that small strokes (transient ischemic attacks) were the only cause, but there are others, such as a narrowing or blockage of blood vessels in the brain. These conditions can result from diabetes and hypertension. Although memory loss occurs later than it does with Alzheimer's disease, other cognitive problems, difficulty walking, and weakness are sometimes experienced. People can also become confused, agitated, or depressed. The symptoms usually progress by steps rather than gradually.

Carrie Hill is a psychologist, a former regional director of the Alzheimer's Association, and the author of many journal articles and book chapters. She is the former About.com expert on Alzheimer's disease.

SOURCE: Carrie Hill, "Vascular Dementia," About.com, June 8, 2010. Copyright © 2012 Carrie Hill (http://alzheimers.about.com). Used with permission of About Inc., which can be found online at www.about.com. All rights reserved.

Vascular dementia results from impaired blood flow to the brain. After Alzheimer's disease, it's one of the most common types of dementia, along with Lewy body dementia. It was formerly called *multi-infarct dementia* because it was thought to only be caused by small strokes. However, the name was changed to *vascular dementia* to reflect the array of conditions that can impair the blood's ability to circulate to the brain. Vascular dementia often occurs alongside Alzheimer's disease, resulting in mixed dementia. Between 1% to 4% of people over the age of 65 have vascular dementia, and the risk of developing it increases dramatically with age.

Vascular dementia can occur either by a narrowing or a complete blockage of blood vessels in the brain, which deprives brain cells from nutrients and oxygen they need to function properly. Vascular dementia often results from several small strokes that occur over time. It can also occur after a single major stroke, which is sometimes referred to as *post-stroke dementia.* Not all strokes lead to dementia, but up to one-third of those who have a stroke will develop dementia within six months. Conditions like high blood pressure and diabetes that don't block blood vessels, but simply narrow them, can also lead to vascular dementia.

People who develop vascular dementia often have a history of one or more of the following: heart attack, stroke, high blood pressure, diabetes, or high cholesterol. In particular, if an individual has a history of multiple strokes, the risk of developing vascular dementia increases with the number of strokes experienced over time.

Symptoms of Vascular Dementia

People with vascular dementia often display multiple cognitive problems, including memory impairment and possibly aphasia [difficulty finding words], apraxia [inability to perform coordinated movements], agnosia [loss of ability to recognize objects], or problems with executive functioning.

In most cases, symptoms make it difficult to hold a job, carry out household responsibilities, or maintain social relationships. People with vascular dementia also experience neurological symptoms such as exaggerated reflexes, problems with walking and balance, and/or weakness in the limbs, hands, and feet. Depending on the individual and on the cause of the dementia, delusions, confusion, agitation, urinary problems, and/or depression can also accompany vascular dementia.

Interestingly, memory loss usually occurs later in the disease compared to when it appears in Alzheimer's. In vascular dementia, the first symptoms are often the neurological ones, such as problems with reflexes, walking, and muscle weakness. On the other hand,

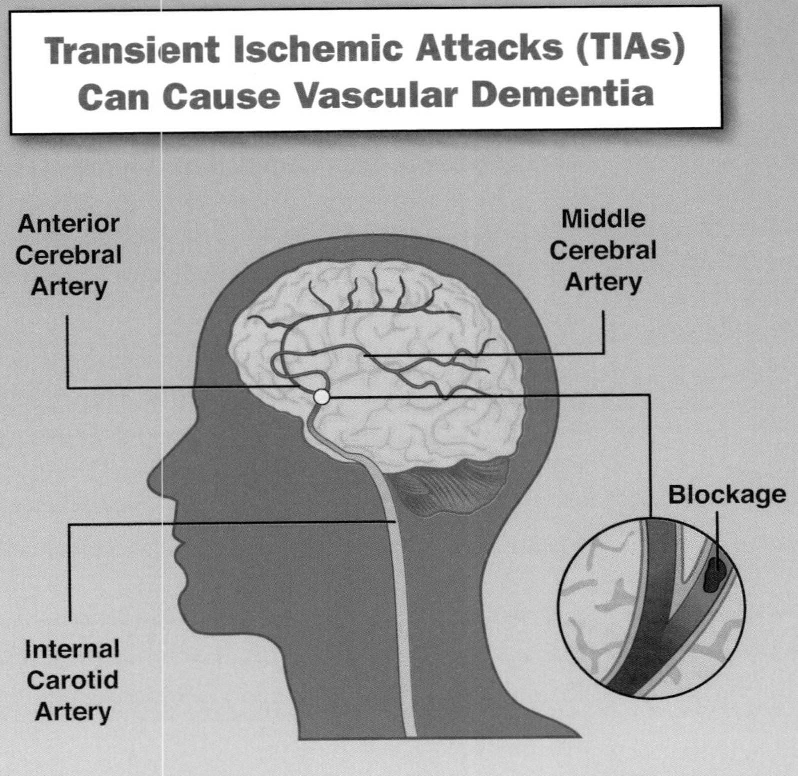

Transient Ischemic Attacks (TIAs) Can Cause Vascular Dementia

Anterior Cerebral Artery

Middle Cerebral Artery

Blockage

Internal Carotid Artery

Taken from: National Stroke Association TIA Brochure. www.stroke.org/site/DocServer/TIA.pdf?docID=405.

memory problems and behavioral symptoms are commonly the first issues noticed in Alzheimer's. Additionally, vascular dementia often progresses in a step-wise fashion. For example, the person will seem stable for a period of time, then suddenly get much worse, then continue to alternate between stable periods and sudden drops in functioning. On the other hand, Alzheimer's disease progresses in a more gradual, downward fashion.

As with Alzheimer's disease, a complete diagnostic workup should be performed in order to rule out other possible causes of the person's symptoms. Vascular dementia is usually identified through imaging procedures, which can reveal strokes and narrowed or blocked arteries. Neuropsychological tests might also be conducted to determine the nature and extent of cognitive impairment.

FAST FACT

There are two subtypes of vascular dementia: multi-infarct dementia, which is caused by strokes, and subcortical dementia, which is caused by a narrowing of blood vessels. Subcortical dementia is also called Binswanger's disease.

Treatment of Vascular Dementia

No drugs have been approved by the FDA [US Food and Drug Administration] specifically to treat vascular dementia, but medications approved to treat Alzheimer's sometimes help. . . .

Managing cardiovascular problems through medication and/or lifestyle changes may help slow the worsening of vascular dementia symptoms. It's critical to monitor blood pressure, pulse, cholesterol, blood sugar, and weight, all of which impact brain health and the ease of blood flow to the brain.

Behavior management strategies are also useful for handling the challenging behaviors that sometimes accompany vascular dementia.

Currently, there is no cure for vascular dementia. If the dementia was caused by multiple strokes, the person

People with vascular dementia often display multiple cognitive problems, including memory impairment and aphasia, or difficulty speaking. (© Tim Vernon, LTH NHS Trust/Photo Researchers, Inc.)

may get worse in a step-wise progression, where stable periods are interrupted by sudden downward episodes. Life expectancy for someone with vascular dementia is highly individual and depends on the nature of the cardiovascular problems that are causing the dementia, along with the person's age and other medical conditions.

Dementia with Lewy Bodies Includes Neuromuscular as Well as Cognitive Symptoms

Family Caregiver Alliance

Dementia with Lewy bodies (DLB—often called Lewy body dementia, or LBD) is similar in many ways to Alzheimer's disease and Parkinson's disease, which are better known; it is therefore hard to diagnose. It is the second most common form of dementia (not counting vascular dementia, which does not involve neurodegenerative brain damage). The nerve cells in the brains of people with DLB contain microscopic round protein lumps called Lewy bodies, which cannot be directly detected until autopsy after death. Doctors therefore use a variety of neurology and psychoneurological tests to distinguish DLB from other disorders. Besides fluctuating mental disability, DLB patients have neuromuscular symptoms, sleep disorders, and frequent hallucinations.

The Family Caregiver Alliance is a community-based nonprofit organization that serves the needs of families and friends providing long-term care at home.

SOURCE: "Dementia with Lewy Bodies," Family Caregiver Alliance, 2010. http://www.caregiver.org. Copyright © 2010 by Family Caregiver Alliance. All rights reserved. Reproduced by permission.

Dementia with Lewy Bodies (DLB) is a progressive degenerative disease or syndrome of the brain. It shares symptoms—and sometimes overlaps—with several diseases, especially Alzheimer's and Parkinson's.

People who develop DLB have behavioral and memory symptoms of dementia like those of Alzheimer's Disease and, to varying extents, the physical, motor system symptoms seen in Parkinson's Disease. However, the mental symptoms of a person with DLB might fluctuate frequently, motor symptoms are milder than for Parkinson's, and DLB patients usually have vivid visual hallucinations.

Dementia with Lewy Body (DLB) is also called "Lewy Body Dementia" (LBD), "Diffuse Lewy Body Disease", "Lewy Body Disease", "Cortical Lewy Body Disease", "Lewy Body Variant of Alzheimer's Disease" or "Parkinson's Disease Dementia." It is the second most common dementia, accounting for 20% of those with dementia (Alzheimer's Disease is first). Dementia is a gradual, progressive decline in mental ability (cognition) that affects memory, thinking processes, behavior and physical activity. In addition to these mental symptoms, persons with DLB experience physical symptoms of parkinsonism, including mild tremor, muscle stiffness and movement problems. Strong visual hallucinations also occur.

DLB is named after smooth round protein lumps (alpha-synuclein) called Lewy bodies, that are found in the nerve cells of the affected parts of the brain. These "abnormal protein structures" were first described in 1912 by Frederich Heimlich Lewy, M.D., a contemporary of Alois Alzheimer who first identified the more common form of dementia that bears his name.

Lewy bodies are found throughout the outer layer of the brain (the cerebral cortex) and deep inside the midbrain and brainstem. They are often found in those diagnosed with Alzheimer's, Parkinson's, Down syndrome and other disorders.

This computer art shows neurons (in blue) containing Lewy bodies (in red). Lewy bodies are deposits of protein found in neurons in the brains of patients with Alzheimer's and Parkinson's disease. (© David Mack/Photo Researchers, Inc.)

The cause of DLB is unknown and no specific risk factors are identified. Cases have appeared among families but there does not seem to be a strong tendency for inheriting the disease. Genetic research may reveal more information about causes and risk in the future. It usually occurs in older adults between 50–85 years old and slightly more men than women have the disease.

Symptoms of Dementia with Lewy Bodies

Initial symptoms of DLB usually are similar to those of Alzheimer's or Vascular Dementia and are cognitive in nature, such as acute confusion, loss of memory, and poor judgment. Other patients may first show the neuromuscular symptoms of parkinsonism—loss of spontaneous movement, rigidity (muscles feel stiff and resist movement), and shuffling gait, while still others may have visual hallucinations as the first symptom. Patients may also suffer from delusions or depression.

Key symptoms are:

- Problems with recent memory such as forgetting recent events.
- Brief episodes of unexplained confusion and other behavioral or cognitive problems. The individual may become disoriented to the time or location where he or she is, have trouble with speech, have difficulty finding words or following a conversation, experience visuospatial difficulty (for example, finding one's way), and have problems in thinking such as inattention, mental inflexibility, indecisiveness, lack of judgment, lack of initiative and loss of insight.
- Fluctuation in the occurrence of cognitive symptoms from moment to moment, hour to hour, day to day or week to week. For example, the person may converse normally one day and be mute and unable to speak the next day. There are also fluctuations in attention, alertness and wakefulness.
- Well defined, vivid, recurrent visual hallucinations. These hallucinations are well formed and detailed. In DLB's early stage, the person may even acknowledge and describe the hallucinations. They are generally benign and patients are not scared by them. Hallucinations may also be auditory (hearing sounds), olfactory (smelling or tasting something) or tactile (feeling or touching something that is not there).
- Movement problems of parkinsonism, sometimes referred to as "extrapyramidal" signs. These symptoms often seem to start spontaneously and may include flexed posture, shuffling gait, muscle jerks or twitches, reduced arm swing, loss of dexterity, limb stiffness, a tendency to fall, balance problems, bradykinesia (slowness of movement), tremor, shakiness, and lack of facial expression.

• Rapid Eye Movement Sleep Behavior Disorder. This is characterized by vivid dreaming, talking in one's sleep, and excessive movement while asleep, including occasionally hitting a bed partner. The result may be excessive daytime drowsiness and this symptom may appear years before DLB is diagnosed. About 50% of patients have this symptom.

Movement and motor problems occur in later stages for 70% of persons with DLB. But for 30% of DLB patients, and more commonly those that are older, Parkinson's symptoms occur first, before dementia symptoms. In these individuals, cognitive decline tends to start with depression or mild forgetfulness.

Brain Cells Containing Lewy Bodies

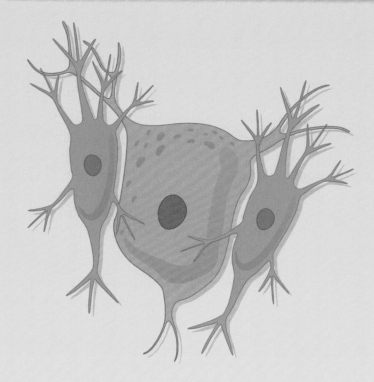

Dementia with Lewy bodies is difficult to diagnose. Not only does it resemble other dementias, it overlaps with Alzheimer's, Parkinson's and other disorders which may result in it being difficult to rule out or exclude. Because no single test exists to diagnose DLB, a variety of medical, neurological and neuropsychological tests are used to pinpoint it and its possible overlap with other illnesses. A definitive diagnosis can only be made by an autopsy at death. There are no medications currently approved to specifically treat DLB. . . .

Alzheimer's and Parkinson's: Differences and Overlap with DLB

DLB's similarity to Alzheimer's and Parkinson's diseases and the fact that Lewy bodies are often found in the brains of patients with these diseases means that clinicians must pay close attention to the factors that distinguish DLB:

FAST FACT

Although Lewy body dementia affects slightly more men than women, far more women than men have Alzheimer's disease or vascular dementia. This is because the risk of developing these two conditions increases with age and, on average, women live longer than men.

- Memory and other cognitive problems occur in both DLB and Alzheimer's. However, in DLB they fluctuate frequently.
- DLB patients experience more depression than do Alzheimer's patients.
- Hallucinations are experienced by Alzheimer's patients in late stages, and by Parkinson's patients who take medications to improve movement and tremor. In DLB, hallucinations occur in early stages, and they are frequent, vivid and detailed.
- Neuroleptic drugs (sometimes called psychotropic drugs) prescribed to lessen the so-called psychiatric symptoms of dementia, such as hallucinations, agitation or restlessness will induce Parkinson's in some DLB patients.
- Life expectancy is slightly shorter for DLB than for Alzheimer's patients.

- At autopsy the brains of DLB patients have senile plaques, a hallmark of Alzheimer's. Another Alzheimer's feature, neurofibrillary tangles, are absent or found in fewer numbers and are concentrated in the neocortex. Other Alzheimer's features—regional neuronal loss, spongiform change and synapse loss, neurochemical abnormalities and neurotransmitter deficits—are also seen. However, DLB-afflicted brains are less damaged than are Alzheimer's brains.
- In DLB movement problems are spontaneous; the symptoms begin suddenly.
- Tremor is less pronounced in DLB than in Parkinson's. Also, DLB patients respond less dramatically to drugs such as Levodopa that are used to treat Parkinson's. Nerve cell loss in the subtantia nigra is not as severe in DLB. Both DLB and Parkinson's patients may sometimes experience fainting and wide alterations in blood pressure. Some Parkinson's patients develop dementia in later stages. Dementia is usually the presenting symptom in DLB.
- Parkinson's patients lose the neurotransmitter dopamine; Alzheimer's patients lose the neurotransmitter acetylcholine. DLB patients lose both.
- In DLB, Alzheimer-like and Parkinson-like symptoms appear within one year of each other.

Despite these differences, a diagnosis of Dementia with Lewy Bodies does not preclude a positive diagnosis of Alzheimer's, Parkinson's or other diseases common in older age.

With an average lifespan after onset of 5 to 7 years, the progress of Dementia with Lewy Bodies is relentless; however, the rate of decline varies with each person. DLB does not follow a pattern of stages as is seen in some other dementias. Death usually occurs from pneumonia or other illness. There is neither cure nor specific treatment to arrest the course of the disease.

Caution must be used in treating a person with DLB. Medications must be monitored closely for proper balance because some patients are adversely affected by some drugs. . . .

Caregiving and DLB

DLB patients can live at home with frequent reassessment and careful monitoring and supervision. Caregivers must watch patients closely because of the tendency for them to fall or lose consciousness. Particular care should be taken when a patient is standing up from a chair or getting out of bed, as blood pressure can drop, causing the patient to lose his or her balance. Dementia prevents patients from learning new actions that might help them overcome movement problems, such as learning to use a walker. They may need more assistance some days than others, and can be reassured by a caregiver's help in turning attention away from the hallucinations.

Caregivers must learn to navigate both skills in dealing with cognitive, behavioral and motor disabilities. Attending support groups and learning skills in how to communicate with someone with dementia as well as learning skills in helping someone with a motor disorder will reduce caregiver stress and frustration.

Frontotemporal Degeneration Occurs More Often than Most Other Dementias in Younger People

Association for Frontotemporal Degeneration

Unlike most types of dementia, frontotemporal degeneration (also called frontotemporal dementia or FTD) generally begins in middle age, although it does strike some elderly people and even a few youthful people. It affects only the frontal and temporal lobes of the brain and can now be diagnosed by brain imaging techniques. Although the symptoms are similar to those of Alzheimer's disease, they begin with behavior problems and language dysfunction rather than memory loss. Deterioration of functioning and thinking ability is progressive and cannot be slowed by treatment. There are a number of different forms of the disease, depending on the areas of the brain affected and on which symptoms predominate. The form known as Pick's disease is characterized by increasingly inappropriate behavior.

The Association for Frontotemporal Degeneration is a nonprofit organization that provides information to frontotemporal degeneration patients and caregivers and advocates for research funding.

SOURCE: "Frontotemporal Degeneration," Association for Frontotemporal Degeneration, 2011. http://www.theaftd.org. Copyright © 2011 by Association for Frontotemporal Degeneration. All rights reserved. Reproduced by permission.

Frontotemporal degeneration (FTD) is a disease process that results in progressive damage to the anterior temporal and/or frontal lobes of the brain. It causes a group of brain disorders that share many clinical features. The hallmark of FTD is a gradual, progressive decline in behavior and/or language that often has a relatively young age at onset (mid-50s to 60s), but has been seen as early as 21 and as late as 80 years. As the disease progresses, it becomes increasingly difficult for people to plan or organize activities, behave appropriately in social or work settings, interact with others, and care for oneself, resulting in increasing dependency.

FTD represents an estimated 10%–20% of all dementia cases and is recognized as one of the most common dementias affecting a younger population. It is estimated that FTD affects approximately 50,000–60,000 Americans. FTD occurs equally in men and women. In a small percentage of cases, it is inherited.

While there are currently no treatments to slow or stop the progression of the disease, FTD research is expanding, producing greater understanding of the disorders. We anticipate that this knowledge will result in a growing number of potential therapeutics entering clinical testing within the next few years.

Historically, physicians had a difficult time distinguishing FTD from Alzheimer's disease (AD), and several other neurological disorders or psychiatric problems. Today, increased understanding of the clinical features and sophisticated brain imaging techniques help the physician to make an accurate diagnosis. Both FTD and AD are characterized by atrophy of the brain, and a gradual, progressive loss of brain function. Frontotemporal degeneration, however, is primarily a disease of behavior and language dysfunction, while the hallmark of AD is loss of memory. FTD often begins at an earlier age than AD; roughly 60% of cases occur in people 45–64 years old.

Symptoms of FTD

The frontal lobes of the brain are associated with decision making and control of behavior, and the temporal lobes with emotion and language. While FTD is marked by a range of behavioral, personality, and cognitive changes, several subtypes of the disorder have been identified based on distinct symptoms and clinical presentation.

Frontotemporal degeneration characterized by loss of empathy and increasingly inappropriate social behavior is known clinically as behavioral variant FTD (bvFTD), Pick's disease, or frontal variant FTD (fvFTD). When problems in language are prominent, the clinical syndrome is known as primary progressive aphasia (PPA). FTD with motor neuron disease, corticobasal syndrome, and progressive supranuclear palsy are subtypes of FTD characterized by muscle weakness, rigidity and/or parkinsonian symptoms.

Behavioral changes are typically seen as changes in personality, emotional blunting or loss of empathy that result in increasingly inappropriate social behavior. People gradually become less involved in routine daily activities and withdraw emotionally from others. Despite acting this way at home, they may also become disinhibited when in public or with strangers. Unusual behaviors may include swearing, overeating (especially carbohydrates) or drinking, impulsivity, shoplifting, hypersexual behavior and deterioration in personal hygiene habits. Accompanying this is a decreasing self-awareness: the patient displays little insight into how inappropriate his or her behavior is, and little or no concern for its effect on other people, including family and friends. Patients may also display repetitive, stereotyped behaviors, such as hand clapping, humming the same song over and over, or walking to the same place day after day.

Language deficits experienced by FTD patients are distinguished by principally two presenting issues: problems with expression of language and problems with word meaning. People with nonfluent/agrammatic PPA become hesitant in their speech and begin to talk less, but appear to retain the meaning of words longer. In semantic variant PPA, people experience a progressive deterioration of understanding words and recognizing objects, but retain the ability to produce fluent speech. A third variant, logopenic PPA, is characterized by deterioration in a person's ability to retrieve words.

Problems in motor skills and movement characterize two frontotemporal disorders. Corticobasal syndrome (CBS) begins with a decrease in movement on one side of the body and muscle rigidity with a tremor. Progressive

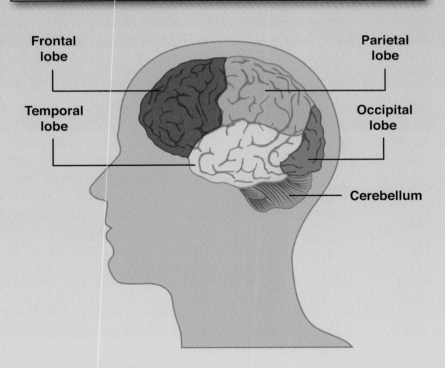

Frontotemporal Dementia Affects the Frontal and Temporal Lobes of the Brain

Frontal lobe

Temporal lobe

Parietal lobe

Occipital lobe

Cerebellum

Taken from: Association for Frontotemporal Degeneration. www.theaftd.org/frontotemporal-degeneration/ftd-overview.

supranuclear palsy (PSP) causes problems with control of gait and balance. The inability to coordinate eye movements is a characteristic symptom of PSP. Problems similar to those seen in Parkinson's disease or ALS may also be seen.

Cognitive and Emotional Disabilities

Damage to the brain's frontal and temporal lobes affect complex thinking and reasoning abilities which can result in other symptoms commonly associated with FTD. Increasing impairment in "executive functions" affects a person's ability to plan, organize and execute activities, while emotional changes impact relationships. Symptoms may include:

- Distractibility and impersistence, increasing difficulty staying on task mentally.
- Mental rigidity and inflexibility, insistence on having his or her own way, increasing difficulty adapting to new or changing circumstances.
- Planning and problem solving impairments, abstract reasoning decreases. Examples of this would include difficulty coordinating the cooking of a meal or making a shopping list and performing necessary errands.
- Poor financial judgment, impulsive spending or financial risk-taking.
- Emotional blunting or abnormal emotional reactions to others. Examples would include being inappropriately calm when a significant other has been hurt or is threatened, or being unfeeling or self-centered when empathy would usually be called for (such as a funeral). Some show emotions that may be exaggerated or inappropriate for the circumstance.
- Apathy, reduced initiative, lack of motivation and an apparent loss of interest in previously-enjoyed hobbies and social activities.

• Lack of insight into one's behavior develops early; the patient does not recognize changes in his or her own behaviors and shows no concern for the effect of these behaviors on others, including loved ones.
• Mood changes that can be abrupt and frequent. . . .

In the majority of cases, FTD is sporadic, meaning it is a disorder that develops in that person by chance rather than being inherited. When FTD is diagnosed in a patient with no family history of FTD or dementia, it is often an isolated (sporadic) case, which appears to pose no significant elevated risk to family members. In a significant minority of FTD patients, a family history suggests a hereditary condition with an autosomal dominant pattern of inheritance. This means there is a clear pattern of FTD-type diagnoses being passed from parent to child, with virtually every patient having an affected parent and each child of an affected person having a 50% chance to inherit the disorder.

Treatment of FTD

There is no cure for FTD and in most cases its progression cannot be slowed. Although no medications have been proven effective specifically for FTD, many clinicians look to the medications and treatment approaches used in other, similar disorders to develop a therapeutic approach. . . .

Although specific symptoms may vary from patient to patient, FTD is marked by an inevitable progressive deterioration in functioning. The length of progression varies, from 2 to over 20 years with a mean course of 8 years from the onset of symptoms. FTD itself is not life-threatening. It does, however, predispose patients to serious complications such as pneumonia, infection, or injury from a fall. The most common cause of death is pneumonia.

FAST FACT

Researchers have found that some frontotemporal dementia patients develop new creative skills in music and art. These talents emerge when brain cell loss occurs predominantly in the left frontal lobe, which controls functions such as language, thus allowing the right frontal lobe to take over.

A colored magnetic resonance imaging (MRI) scan shows a brain with frontotemporal dementia. The frontal lobe, left, and temporal lobe, center, have atrophied, or shrunk. (© Zephyr/Photo Researchers, Inc.)

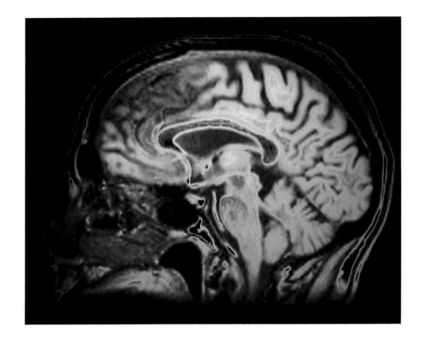

It is important for caregivers and families to think about long-term management issues and identify a team of experts who can help with difficult medical, financial and emotional challenges. It is imperative to have a physician who is knowledgeable about FTD and approaches to treatment. Other medical specialists who may be helpful include: speech and language pathologists, occupational and physical therapists, neuropsychologists, nurses (especially home-care nursing), social workers and genetic counselors. . . .

It is also important to consider the type of care situations that may be necessary during later stages of the disease. In-home nursing care, transition to life-care community or a nursing home are three such options. When plans are made ahead of time they can afford the family a smoother transition and allow the patient to be involved in the decision-making process if he/she is capable.

The World Health Organization Expects Dementia Cases to Triple by 2050

Frank Jordans

The World Health Organization issued a special report in April 2012 warning about the growing problem of dementia. The number of people in the world who have it is expected to double by 2030 and triple by the middle of the century. Most people with dementia are cared for by relatives, many of whom are driven below the poverty line by the financial burden. Dementia is already a major public health issue in rich countries, but the number of cases will rise even faster in poor and middle-income countries, where population is rapidly increasing, improved medical care is keeping people alive longer, and there is little public awareness of the problem. Often dementia is mistakenly thought to be a normal part of aging and is overlooked, and people who have it do not receive adequate care.

Frank Jordans is a writer for the Associated Press.

SOURCE: Frank Jordans, "WHO: Dementia Cases Worldwide Will Triple by 2050," *Seattle Post- Intelligencer*, April 11, 2012. Copyright © 2012 by the Associated Press. All rights reserved. Reproduced by permission.

Cases of dementia—and the heavy social and financial burdens associated with them—are set to soar in the coming decades as life expectancy and medical care improve in poorer countries, the World Health Organization [WHO] says.

Some 35.6 million people were living with dementia in 2010, but that figure is set to double to 65.7 million by 2030, the U.N. health agency said Wednesday [April 11, 2012]. In 2050, it expects dementia cases to triple to 115.4 million.

"The numbers are already large and are increasing rather rapidly," said Dr. Shekhar Saxena, the head of WHO's mental health division.

Most dementia patients are cared for by relatives who shoulder the bulk of the current estimated annual cost of $604 billion. And the financial burden is expected to rise even faster than the number of cases, WHO said in its first substantial report on the issue.

"The catastrophic cost drives millions of households below the poverty line," warned the agency's director-general, Margaret Chan.

Dementia, a brain illness that affects memory, behavior and the ability to perform even common tasks, affects mostly older people. About 70 percent of cases are believed to be caused by Alzheimer's.

In the last few decades, dementia has become a major public health issue in rich countries. But with populations in poor and middle-income countries projected to grow and age rapidly over the coming decades, WHO appealed for greater public awareness and better support programs everywhere.

The share of cases in poor and middle-income countries is expected to rise from just under 60 percent today, to over 70 percent by 2050.

So far, only eight countries—including Britain, France and Japan—have national programs to address dementia,

FAST FACT

Because of the growing number of people over age sixty-five, the number of new dementia cases per year in the United States is expected to double by 2050. In 2012 someone in America developed Alzheimer's disease every sixty-eight seconds; by midcentury someone will develop AD every thirty-three seconds.

WHO said. Several others, such as the United States, have plans at the state level.

While the report shies away from making specific recommendations to policy makers, it does urge them to address the challenges of dementia as soon as possible.

Emerging economies such as China, India and Brazil, for example, have functioning health care systems but don't have the capacity to deal with the massive rise in dementia, said Saxena.

Ensuring doctors and nurses can spot symptoms is a start because lack of proper diagnosis is one of the obstacles to better treatment, he said. Even in rich countries, more than half of dementia cases are overlooked until the disease has reached a late stage, according to the report.

One common misconception is that dementia is inevitable.

"Most people regard dementia as a normal sign of aging, which is not correct," said Saxena.

"Older people have problems of memory and cognition, but dementia is a disease with much more rapid symptoms and progression."

Britain's prime minister, David Cameron, announced on March 26, 2012, that funding for research into dementia would be doubled to the US equivalent of $106 million by 2015. Britain is one of only eight countries that have national programs to address dementia. (© Pool/Reuters/Landov)

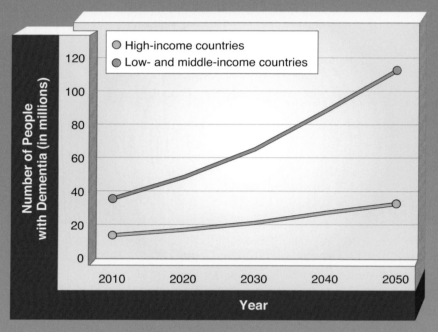

Projected Increase in Number of People with Dementia

Number of People with Dementia (in millions)

- High-income countries
- Low- and middle-income countries

120

100

80

60

40

20

0

2010   2020   2030   2040   2050

Year

Taken from: World Health Organization, *Dementia: A Public Health Priority*, April 2012. http://whqlibdoc.who.int/publications/2012/9789241564458_eng.pdf.

Badly treated or ignored, dementia sufferers can become isolated and vulnerable, especially if they also have poor eyesight or hearing.

And rich countries like the United States should reconsider the drive to place dementia patients in institutions, said Saxena. "That's a mistake that some developed countries have made that is neither financially viable nor providing the best care," he said.

To Saxena, the increasing rate of dementia is a "paradox" of medical progress.

"The better we do, the more we expect to have problems with dementia and we need to be prepared for that," he said.

The US Government Is Seeking Better Ways of Caring for People with Dementia

Lauran Neergaard

The US government is developing a national plan to deal with Alzheimer's disease, hoping to find effective treatments and improve support for patients and caregivers by 2025. Some believe that a way can be found to delay its onset if not completely prevent it, but the highest priority is to help the 5.4 million Americans who already have dementia, a figure expected to rise to 16 million by the middle of the century. It is expected that medical and nursing home costs will reach $13 trillion by 2050, not counting the care provided by relatives and friends. The plan aims to increase public awareness of dementia's early warning signs, give doctors tools to assess them, have caregivers' health regularly checked, and improve support for families. Such programs would cost much less than nursing home care, but the money to implement them has not yet been made available.

Lauran Neergaard is a medical writer for the Associated Press.

SOURCE: Lauran Neergaard, "US Wants Effective Alzheimer's Treatment by 2025," *Boston Globe*, January 17, 2012. Copyright © 2012 by the Associated Press. All rights reserved. Reproduced by permission.

Effective treatments for Alzheimer's by 2025? That's the target the government is eyeing as it develops a national strategy to tackle what could become the defining disease of a rapidly aging population.

It's an ambitious goal—and on Tuesday [January 17, 2012], advisers to the government stressed that millions of families need better help now to care for their loved ones.

"What's really important here is a comprehensive plan that deals with the needs of people who already have the disease," said Alzheimer's Association president Harry Johns, one of the advisers.

Already families approach the advisory committee "reminding us of the enormity of our task," said Dr. Ron Petersen, an Alzheimer's specialist at the Mayo Clinic who chairs the panel.

The [Barack] Obama administration is developing the first National Alzheimer's Plan to address the medical and social problems of dementia—not just better treatments but better day-to-day care for dementia patients and their overwhelmed caregivers, too.

FAST FACT

In 2008, 42 percent of the Medicare recipients diagnosed with dementia lived in a nursing home or assisted living facility, 44 percent lived in the community with another person, and 15 percent lived alone.

The plan still is being written, with the advisory panel's input. But a draft of its overall goals sets 2025 as a target date to have effective treatments and ways to delay if not completely prevent the illness.

Some advisory members said that's not aggressive enough, and 2020 would be a better target date.

"We want to be bold," said Dr. Jennifer Manly of Columbia University. "We think the difference of five years is incredibly meaningful."

Regardless, an estimated 5.4 million Americans already have Alzheimer's or similar dementias—and how to help their families cope with day-to-day care is a priority, the advisory committee made clear Tuesday.

The disease is growing steadily as the population ages: By 2050, 13 million to 16 million Americans are projected to have Alzheimer's, costing $1 trillion in medical and nursing home expenditures. That doesn't count the billions of dollars in unpaid care provided by relatives and friends.

Today's treatments only temporarily ease some dementia symptoms, and work to find better ones has been frustratingly slow. Scientists now know that Alzheimer's is brewing for years before symptoms appear, and they're hunting ways to stall the disease, maybe long enough that potential sufferers will die of something else first. But it's still early-stage work.

Meanwhile, as many as half of today's Alzheimer's sufferers haven't been formally diagnosed, a recent report found. That's in part because of stigma and the belief that nothing can be done. Symptomatic treatment aside, a diagnosis lets families plan, and catching Alzheimer's

Health-care employees in Kansas City, Missouri, attend a seminar to better understand dementia and learn how to better care for dementia patients. (© Fred Blocher/MCT/ Landov)

earlier would be crucial if scientists ever find a way to stall it, the advisory panel noted.

Among the goals being debated for the national plan:

- Begin a national public awareness campaign of dementia's early warning signs, to improve timely diagnosis.
- Give primary care doctors the tools to assess signs of dementia as part of Medicare's annual check-up.
- Have caregivers' health, physical and mental, regularly checked.
- Improve care-planning and training for families so they know what resources are available for their loved one and themselves.

A training program in New York, for instance, has proved that caregivers who are taught how to handle common dementia problems, and given support, are able to keep their loved ones at home for longer.

Such programs "are dirt cheap compared to paying for nursing home care," said David Hoffman, who oversees Alzheimer's programs for the New York State Department of Health.

But hanging over the meeting was the reality of a budget crunch. The government hasn't said how much money it will be able to devote to the Alzheimer's plan, and states have seen their own Alzheimer's budgets cut.

"We're not going to fix this without substantial resources," Hoffman said. "In New York, we're hanging on by our nails," he added.

CHAPTER 2

Controversies Concerning Dementia

Myths About Dementia May Be Harmful to Patients

Peter Lin

There are many myths about Alzheimer's disease (AD). In the follow-ing viewpoint Peter Linn explains that one such myth is that signifi-cant cognitive decline is a normal part of aging. Others are that AD is caused by the mercury in dental filings, fish, flu shots, or the alu-minum in cooking utensils. Still another is that it is inherited, when actually only 5 percent of AD cases have a genetic cause. In Lin's opinion, another myth is that there is no treatment; although existing treatments have only modest effects on most patients, he considers them of benefit. He also considers it untrue that there is no point in diagnosis when there is no cure.

Lin is the past medical director of the University of Toronto Health and Wellness Centre, the director of primary care initiatives at the Canadian Heart Research Centre, and the medical director of LinCorp Medical in Toronto, Ontario.

Photo on previous page. A woman with Alzheimer's holds a photo of her family, whom she cannot remember. (© Angela Hampton Picture Library/ Alamy)

SOURCE: Peter Lin, "Myths in the Media," *Canadian Review of Alzheimer's Disease and Other Dementias,* October 2010, pp. 23–26. Copyright © 2010 by Peter J. Lin. All rights reserved. Reproduced by permission.

In an attempt to explain the phenomena around them, ancient Greeks created myths of Gods and believed that lightning bolts were controlled by Zeus and raging waves were controlled by Poseidon. Science was eventually able to explain the phenomena and dispel the myths, but only when the data was available to do so. Just as the ancient Greeks, medicine too has many myths or theories that attempt to explain what we do not yet understand. These myths, however, can be harmful, affecting our ability to care for our patients, such as determining whether to treat a condition or screen for a disease, and must therefore be dispelled. For example, it was once believed that blood pressure needed to rise with age in order to ensure a continuous blood flow through clogging arteries. This belief deterred healthcare professionals from treating blood pressure for decades by implying that lowering blood pressure would cause lack of flow and cause strokes. Clinical trials later disproved this theory by showing lower blood pressure helped to reduce the risk of stroke and heart attacks.

Many theories have circulated in the field of Alzheimer's disease (AD) as well and, over time, some have been disproved and are now considered myths. But the label of myth is more than just a disproved theory. A myth is where the majority of the people (public) still have the belief despite evidence that disproves it. In this brief article, a collection of the more common myths will be reviewed.

Myth 1: It Is Just Normal Aging

There is a belief that, just as our joints get stiffer with age, cognitive decline and senility are simply part of the normal aging process. Many patients and physicians believe this theory. The harm in this belief is that it implies that there is no need to identify patients with cognitive decline in order to treat them. This causes a dismissive attitude towards the condition. Doctors often say, "Well, you are 70 years old" and do not pursue the matter further. The truth is there is a decline in cognitive function with age, but the slope is gradual. Patients with AD have a much sharper decline, losing two to four points on the Mini Mental State Examination (MMSE) over a one-year period.

The analogy to rheumatologic patients is quite simple. Just as cognitive function declines with age, so do joint function and cartilage integrity. Patients with rheumatoid arthritis (RA) experience a significantly faster decline due to an accelerated inflammatory process that destroys the joint and cartilage cells. This same concept applies to patients with AD; an accelerated neuronal death leads to a rapid cognitive function decline. Thus, just as RA is not normal aging, we can ascertain that AD is not due to simple aging as well.

By dispelling the myth "It is just normal aging", we become less dismissive and monitor cognitive scores more closely to see if the decline is gradual or rapid in our patients. If the patient has a rapid decline, we can determine it is not normal aging, diagnose AD and propose treatment at an earlier stage, leading to an improved preservation of cognition and function.

Myth 2: Dental Fillings and Flu Shots Cause AD

Dental fillings. The theory that dental fillings caused AD emerged when patients learned there was mercury in the fillings, which has been used for nearly 150 years. Mercury, a heavy metal, is toxic to many organ systems, and the brain is one of its favorite targets. Dental fillings can last for many decades, but there is a possibility that daily chewing can release the fillings' mercury content. Further, patients who grind their teeth or chew gum regularly have an increased risk of exposure. This news garnered a lot of media attention and some dentists advocated the removal of the fillings.

Unfortunately, drilling these fillings out actually released significantly more mercury and raised the short-term mercury levels in patients. The American Dental Association (ADA) has clearly stated there is no direct connection between mercury and AD. Interestingly, dentists and dental staff have higher levels of mercury due to their exposure at work, but there was no excessive increase of AD in this population.

Another common source of mercury is fish. However, there was no increased rate of AD present in countries where fish is a diet staple, such as Japan. Though there is an increased exposure to mercury through fillings and fish, Health Canada states there is no increased rate of AD when exposed.

Flu shots. It was once believed that flu shots also caused AD. Thimerosal, which contains mercury, is used as a preservative in the multidose vials of flu vaccines. Flu shots are traditionally given to patients older than 65

The number one myth about dementia is that it is just part of the aging process, which has caused some people and even some doctors to take a dismissive attitude toward it. (© **Nic Cleave/ Alamy**) years in the majority of cases. This is also the same age that symptoms of AD begin to present. The coincidence of the flu shot and the AD symptoms led many to believe that the mercury in the shots had caused AD.

However, in 2001, as part of the *Canadian Study of Health and Aging*, 3,682 patients were assessed with regards to previous vaccinations and AD. The investigators studied previous exposures to diphtheria, tetanus, polio and influenza vaccines, and did not find an increase in AD. Rather, there was a reduction in AD rates in patients who had had these vaccinations.

Also, in the Netherlands, 26,071 patients older than 65 years of age were studied to determine the effect of influenza vaccines on death. The results showed that for patients who had regular vaccines, there was a 24% reduction in mortality. According to the results of these studies, we can ascertain that the flu vaccine does not seem to cause AD, but is helpful in preventing death. Therefore, this myth is of great concern because if left unchallenged, patients may not get their annual flu shot and miss out on the protection it can provide.

Myth 3: Aluminum Causes AD

Another media sensation occurred when it was reported that using aluminum pots or drinking from aluminum containers could lead to AD; a myth that was formed based on several findings. In 1975, researchers injected aluminum intraventricularly into rabbit brains, causing the formation of neurofibrillary tangles. Although these tangles were not the same as the tangles found in AD, it was suggested that this could be an animal model of AD. In addition, some studies found that in patients with AD at autopsy, neurons with neurofibrillary tangles had higher amounts of aluminum and amyloid plaques had aluminum inside the plaques themselves. Thus, it was suggested that aluminum causes AD. This theory was later disproved with nuclear microscopy tests which did not find aluminum inside neurons or plaques, but did show an increase in iron, phosphorus and sulfur. In fact, the aluminum that the original researchers had seen were most likely a contaminant, which resulted from how the tissue samples had been processed. Thus, the connection to tinfoil and aluminum pots was lost and with it, the simple prevention strategy of removing aluminum vanished into the realm of myths.

Myth 4: No Family Members Have AD, I Will Not Get It

Familial AD (FAD). This myth is often asked in reverse, "If my mother has AD, does it mean I will get it too?" Essentially, patients are asking what is the genetic component of AD and how they will be affected. The familial type, which tends to strike early, accounts for only about 5% of cases of AD according to the National Institute of Aging (NIA). The genetic defects of patients with familial AD (FAD) are present on chromosome 1, 14 or 21, and each of these defects (mutations) lead to the formation of specific abnormal proteins. . . .

These defects are inherited in an autosomal dominant fashion; the children have a 50/50 chance of developing this early disease.

Fortunately, the majority of AD cases are not FAD, but the sporadic type that tends to occur later in life. If patients in the latter group have a first degree relative with AD, they have an increased risk of having AD as well, but not as dramatically as the true familial type.

Genetic risk factors. There are many risk factors for sporadic cases or late onset AD, such as cardiovascular (*e.g.*, hypertension and diabetes) and genetics.

In order to look for the genetic risk, ApoE4 testing became of interest. ApoE proteins are located on particles that carry cholesterol and triglycerides in the blood stream. . . .

> **FAST FACT**
>
> Alzheimer's disease is the sixth leading cause of death in the United States and the fifth-leading cause for people over age sixty-five.

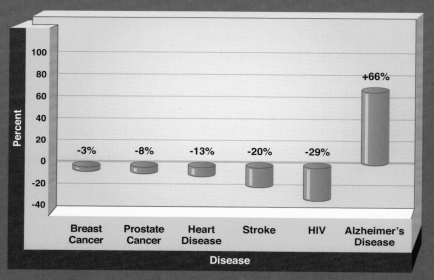

Changing Causes of Death Between 2000 and 2008

Deaths from Alzheimer's disease increased by 66 percent between 2000 and 2008, while deaths from other major diseases declined. This was because other diseases can be treated more effectively than in the past, so people who otherwise would have died from them lived long enough to get AD.

Percent

-3%	-8%	-13%	-20%	-29%	+66%
Breast Cancer	Prostate Cancer	Heart Disease	Stroke	HIV	Alzheimer's Disease

Disease

Taken from: Alzheimer's Association, 2012 Alzheimer's Disease Facts and Figures. www.alz.org/alzheimers_disease_facts_and_figures.asp#quickfacts.

According to the NIA, 40% of late onset AD patients have ApoE4, and it was first believed that the protein would help identify at-risk patients. Unfortunately, more than 30% of the general population have ApoE4, and though the presence of the protein increases the risk of AD, not all will develop the disease. This is an important distinction from FAD where, if you have the gene defect, it is autosomal dominant. Thus, AD occurs in the patient. The presence of ApoE4 increases the risk of developing AD, but it is not a certainty that the patient will have AD. This situation is analogous to having high blood pressure, which increases the risk of having a heart attack. However, many people who have high blood pressure will never have one.

Further, because patients can now order kits to test for ApoE, it is important to ensure that they understand that a positive test means they have an increased risk of AD, but will not necessarily have AD.

Myth 5: There Is No Treatment or Cure

The exact sequence of events in AD are not well understood and many unanswered questions remain, including whether it's the amyloid plaques that kill the neurons; or if neurofibrillary tangles inside the neurons that disrupt movement of nutrients inside the cell kills the neurons and forms the plaques; or if oxidative stress on the neuron is the initial insult and the plaques and tangles are the result. Only when we understand the sequence and mechanisms of the disease will we be able to create a cure.

However, it is known that acetylcholine (ACh) neurons in patients with AD are damaged, and that medications that boost ACh signals can be helpful. Though we cannot inject ACh directly into the brain, we can block the breakdown of the ACh that is released. This will allow the ACh signaling from the remaining neurons to stay on longer and, hence, maintain function. . . .

Though the benefits of current treatments are often modest in their effects, patients and family members do benefit from these treatments. Some patients may even have dramatic improvements (*i.e.*, the so-called "super responders"), while others become stabilized and have a reduced rate of decline. Thus, although the exact mechanism is not clear and there is no cure, support for the injured neurons in the brain can still be of use to patients.

Myth 6: If There Is No Cure, Why Make a Diagnosis?

Many people wonder if there is no cure for AD, why bother with a diagnosis? It is interesting that in diabetes and hypertension there is no cure either, yet the therapies are still viewed as valuable. In AD, the therapies are providing support to the ailing neurons by boosting their signal, and that too should be viewed as valuable.

Medical and social protection. It is also important to diagnose AD early so that physicians and family members can take the necessary steps to protect the patient medically and socially. For example, if a healthcare professional is unaware that his or her patient has AD and that patient is prescribed warfarin for atrial fibrillation and forgets to take his medication, the results could be disastrous. Thus, it is critical to diagnose the patient in order to treat the other medical conditions safely and effectively. In order to ensure that no inappropriate decisions are made on behalf of the patient and to protect the patient's rights, proper legal documentation (*i.e.*, wills and power of attorney) must be completed.

Definitive diagnosis. Many critics have said that a definitive AD diagnosis is hard to make even at autopsy. Some patients may have plaques and tangles and no dementia, while others have very little pathology with full blown dementia. Some physicians ask, why are we trying to make a diagnosis if we are not even certain at autopsy? It is in fact the imprecise nature of the disease that illustrates why we must determine how to best diagnose AD. By knowing the patient and how they have changed, and by talking to the caregivers, we can piece together evidence and make the diagnosis of AD. Initially, AD is a slow progressive decline in cognition, which then spreads to include function and behavior— all clues that help us make a "probable diagnosis of AD." In cardiology, the exact cause of heart attacks were not known for many decades, yet patients were diagnosed and treated for their condition. The same should be said for AD. We must use what clinical skills we have to make the diagnosis and move the patient forward in the best way possible.

Myth 7: All the New Drugs Have Failed

There is always a sense of disappointment when new agents fail to meet expectations during tests. Each negative trial, however, allows us to strike off that particular strategy and to hone in on alternative strategies, giving us insight into areas that may be more successful. For example, there is now hope testing oxidative stress pathways and insulin resistance in the brain. Failures are not true failures, but necessary steps on the path to discovering treatments. Unfortunately, human clinical trials take a long time to complete. Ideally, the efforts in the AD field should be doubled in order to investigate the possibilities at a faster pace.

Myths will always linger as they are cast up as explanations for that which we do not know. They will come and go, some becoming engrained in the public's mind despite data that say otherwise. Before great efforts are expended in dispelling these myths, physicians must take a step back and see which are causing harm; these must be targeted and targeted well. The others that cause no harm can be left to fade into our memories.

As we move forward, our standards of diagnosis and treatment will improve and, one day, our time will be known as the archaic era in which physicians struggled to diagnose and treat AD with no available cure. Though we all look forward to that day, we must use what we know to provide our patients with the best care possible today.

Social Stigma Hurts People with Dementia and Their Families

World Health Organization

The World Health Organization (WHO), in this excerpt from a recent report, points out that dementia is not understood by the public. It is often viewed as a normal part of aging rather than a disease process. On the other hand, in some countries its symptoms are thought to be caused by evil spirits or witchcraft. In the United States and many European nations, it is people's greatest health fear apart from cancer. The very word *dementia* has a negative connotation, and in most places there is social stigma attached to it—which extends to caregivers. Therefore, WHO believes there should be a campaign to raise public awareness, emphasizing understanding, reduction of stigma and discrimination, early diagnosis, living well with dementia, and reducing risk through healthy living.

WHO is the directing and coordinating authority for health within the United Nations system.

SOURCE: "Public Understanding of Dementia: From Awareness to Acceptance," *Dementia: A Public Health Priority*, World Health Organization, April 2012. Copyright © 2012 by the World Health Organization. All rights reserved. Reproduced by permission.

Many people know someone affected by dementia. However, despite rising awareness of dementia, understanding of the syndrome is low. Dementia is often considered to be a natural part of ageing. Sometimes the symptoms are misunderstood as being caused by evil spirits.

The lack of understanding contributes to fears about developing dementia and fosters stigmatizing practices such as avoidance or discrimination. For those who have dementia and for their caregivers and families, the stigma contributes to social isolation and to delays in seeking a diagnosis and help.

This chapter examines awareness, knowledge and attitudes to dementia within society. It is imperative that public awareness and understanding is enhanced in order to reduce the stigma associated with dementia and to enable people with dementia and their caregivers to access support at the appropriate time. Processes for supporting a move towards acceptance of dementia are outlined and illustrated with examples of public and political campaigns to support a societal shift towards acceptance and inclusion of dementia and the people who are affected by it.

Awareness and Understanding of Dementia

Several themes emerge from the literature relating to the lack of awareness and understanding of dementia among the public. First, it is often understood to be a normal part of ageing rather than a disease process.

Second, people do not know about or recognize the symptoms of dementia. For example, 81% of respondents of the "Facing Dementia Survey" conducted in Europe believed that most people do not know the difference between the early stages of Alzheimer's disease and behaviour associated with normal ageing.

Finally, there is a lack of understanding of the associated risk factors. As vascular risk factors (including hypertension and high cholesterol) are also likely to be risk factors for dementia, an understanding of this link can encourage lifestyle modifications.

A number of statements on awareness and understanding of dementia in their country were put to the WHO [World Health Organization] dementia survey respondents. There was a marked difference in responses between high-income and LMIC [low and middle-income countries]. There is a greater likelihood that dementia will be understood as "being due to irreversible and progressive diseases of the brain" in high-income countries, while "no or limited awareness of the syndrome" is more likely in LMIC. Two respondents also indicated a difference in understanding between city-dwellers and people living in rural and remote areas.

The Impact of Stigma

Low levels of understanding about dementia contribute to a number of misperceptions about the disease and result in a perpetuation of stigma which is, sadly, prevalent in most countries. Misperception occurs on a number of levels: the broader community, people with dementia and their families, and those who provide health and social services to them.

Lack of understanding of the nature of the condition in the general public contributes to a fear of developing dementia.

In the *Value of Knowing* study conducted by Harvard School of Public Health and Alzheimer Europe in five countries (France, Germany, Poland, Spain and USA) 70% of respondents knew or had known someone with Alzheimer's disease and 30% reported they had a family member with dementia.

Despite this exposure, findings indicate that dementia is the biggest health fear after cancer in four of the five

How the Majority of People in Different Countries Perceive Dementia

Perception	Low- and middle-income countries	High-income countries
There is no or limited awareness of the syndrome dementia or the diseases associated with dementia	86.3%	37.5%
Symptoms of dementia are perceived as a normal part of aging	86.3%	75.0%
Symptoms of dementia are perceived as a sign of mental illness	81.8%	62.5%
The causes of symptoms of dementia are perceived as being linked to supernatural or spiritual beliefs	31.8%	0.0%
There is an understanding of dementia being due to irreversible and progressive diseases of the brain	54.5%	87.5%

Taken from: World Health Organization. "Public Understanding of Dementia: From Awareness to Acceptance." *Dementia: A Public Health Priority*, April 2012. http://whqlibdoc.who.int/publications/2012/9789241564458_eng.pdf.

countries. Similarly, the IMPACT (Important Perspectives on Alzheimer's Care and Treatment) study found that Alzheimer's disease was ranked second out of 10 diseases that people would be most fearful of developing in the future.

Results from the IMPACT study indicated that participants were "somewhat concerned" (40.8% of 1 000) or "very concerned" (31.8% of 1 000) about losing contact with family and friends. This fear is reinforced by the negative or derogatory language that may be used to describe people with dementia. In Japan, where the word for dementia has a negative association, the government officially changed the word for the condition.

Participants in the WHO dementia survey were asked about stigma. Twenty-five of the 30 country respondents indicated that stigma associated with dementia negatively affects people with dementia and family caregivers. Ten respondents explained that people with dementia were isolated or hidden because of shame or because of the potential for behavioural or psychological symptoms to be seen by others.

> **FAST FACT**
>
> Researchers in the United Kingdom are conducting a trial to find out whether stress increases the risk for dementia. They will collect biomarkers that indicate stress every six months from people with mild cognitive impairment and see whether the biomarkers are related to progression of impairment.

Socioeconomic and cultural variables contribute to shaping knowledge and beliefs about dementia. In LMIC, poor recognition and lack of public awareness cause significant problems. Cultural factors such as belief systems influence understanding of and attitudes to dementia. In Togo, for example, symptoms of dementia may be understood as resulting from witchcraft.

People with dementia report that they find it difficult to talk about the disease because they fear the consequences which could include loss of friendships. A belief that nothing can be done leads to feelings of hopelessness which can affect people's wellbeing.

Stigma and discrimination extend to family caregivers. For example, the symptoms experienced by people with dementia, which may include poor self-care or incontinence, are often regarded by others as evidence of neglect. Furthermore, to the extent that individuals attempt to avoid social interactions with people with dementia, family caregivers may be inadvertently excluded as well.

A few studies have reported that people with dementia have found some general practitioners unhelpful or dismissive about dementia and their symptoms. An unhelpful attitude from a service provider clearly contributes to negative perceptions held by persons living with dementia.

Stigma and misunderstanding can have a devastating impact on all stages of a person's journey through dementia, thus demonstrating the need for urgent action to reduce stigma and to raise the level of understanding across all sectors of society.

Awareness-Raising Campaigns

For awareness-raising to be effective, the issues to be addressed must be clearly identified. For example, in the United Kingdom an extensive review of qualitative and quantitative surveys has identified several themes. These are:

- raising public awareness and understanding of dementia;
- reducing the stigma of dementia and challenging discriminatory behaviour;
- recognizing the early signs of dementia to aid early diagnosis;
- living well with dementia;
- the importance of a healthy lifestyle and reducing risk.

Similar themes also emerged from the WHO survey. Examples of campaigns and other means of raising awareness according to the five identified themes are described below.

Theme 1: raising public awareness and understanding of dementia

At the heart of awareness-raising and information is the message that dementia is a disease causing disability and not an inevitable consequence of ageing. Awareness-raising and understanding are important for countering the fatalism and stigma that is often associated with dementia. They may also contribute to the capacity of family caregivers to cope better with looking after relatives with dementia.

There are many examples of campaigns from around the world that aim to raise awareness and understanding of the condition. The 10-year nationwide campaign undertaken in Japan to raise public awareness and understanding is one such example. It is a large-scale campaign initiated by the government and targeting people from all walks of life, including children.

Civil society has a major role to play in awareness-raising campaigns. These campaigns often involve celebrities and, more recently, people with dementia and their caregivers who provide a positive image of living with dementia. A global focus for awareness-raising is World Alzheimer Day (21 September) and World Alzheimer's Month (September), which was started by ADI [Alzheimer's Disease International] in 1994 and has become an annual day in many countries of the world. A number of examples of activities are provided on the ADI web site.

There are few examples of campaigns in LMIC, and still fewer of their effectiveness. One example is the evaluation of responses to the use of a well-known celebrity for a television campaign by the Brazilian Alzheimer Association. The association secured television time and involved a famous actress. The purpose of the campaign was to increase general awareness and, as a result, the number of calls to the helpline rose from 1 000 to 2 400 per month.

Theme 2: reducing the stigma of dementia

The United Kingdom campaign "I have dementia, I also have a life" demonstrates a targeted approach to dispelling fears in one specific group within society. Targeting a 40–60-year-old predominantly female audience, the campaign—which used television, radio, the press and internet—featured people with dementia. The advertising, which aimed to raise levels of understanding, was developed as a result of qualitative research. Although in previous research people with dementia and their families said they felt stigmatized, the results of the qualitative research, which was conducted with people who had little or no experience of dementia, showed that what was being perceived as stigma was something very different.

As part of the Barack Obama administration's efforts to increase public knowledge of dementia, a website, Alzheimers.gov, was launched in May 2012. (© **AP Images/HHS**)

It showed great fear of dementia, fear of getting the condition and fear of engaging with people with dementia. The advertising campaign therefore sought to "normalize" dementia rather than to "medicalize" it since the latter could lead to increased fear.

Theme 3: recognizing the early symptoms to aid in timely diagnosis and initiation of treatment

Many people are not aware of the range of symptoms associated with dementia. They are most likely to view memory loss as a symptom of dementia, rather than other symptoms such as loss of interest or behavioural changes. When people with symptoms, or their families, believe that memory loss is a natural part of ageing they fail to seek medical advice. The health profession has a role to play in this area by actively assessing for symptoms in ageing patients and by providing information to at-risk patients. This is important for raising the awareness of both the general public and the health professionals. The Alzheimer's Association in the USA carried out the "Know the 10 Signs" campaign to raise awareness about the early diagnosis of dementia.

Theme 4: promoting quality of life

Different media channels such as film, television, internet and social media provide opportunities for disseminating positive images and messages about dementia. The documentary film *I remember better when I pain,* for example, sends a powerful message about the abilities that can remain despite the diagnosis.

It also demonstrates the value of activities that provide outlets for expression for people with dementia. Although the empirical evidence is not strong, some research evidence suggests that engagement in creative arts can provide meaningful stimulation, improve social interaction and improve levels of self-esteem.

Theme 5: providing information about risk factors

Factual information can be used in a number of ways to raise the level of understanding across society, including the political arena and people with dementia and their families. In some countries, campaigns that target risk reduction provide information based on best available evidence.

People Without Symptoms Should Not Be Tested for Biomarkers of Alzheimer's Disease

Naomi Freundlich

The National Institutes of Health has stated that there is no evidence of an effective way to prevent Alzheimer's disease (AD). However, new technologies are making it easier to diagnose, and it may soon be possible for tests to identify biomarkers before a person has any symptoms. This is a controversial development because it could double or even triple the number of people diagnosed with AD at the expense of great psychological suffering as well as in public money. At present there are no treatments that can stop dementia from progressing. Furthermore, if widely used, the tests might produce many false positives. Some experts believe the disadvantages of these tests outweigh the benefits. It would do people little good to know in advance that they were going to get a degenerative disease that could not be treated or cured. Therefore, says Naomi Freundlich, tests for biomarkers should be used only for research purposes.

Freundlich is an award-winning journalist who specializes in health-care policy and a former senior research associate at the Century Foundation.

SOURCE: Naomi Freundlich, "Diagnosis Without Treatment: The Perils of New Tests for Early Alzheimer's Disease," *Health Beat*, July 26, 2010. http://www.healthbeatblog.com. Copyright © 2010 by Naomi Freundlich. All rights reserved. Reproduced by permission.

In April [2010], an independent panel established by the National Institutes of Health came to the disheartening conclusion that currently, there is nothing to prevent or delay the progress of Alzheimer's disease in those of us who are destined to join the 5 million Americans currently suffering from this dreaded ailment.

The panel found that: "Although numerous interventions have been suggested to delay Alzheimer's disease, the evidence is inadequate to conclude that any are effective." Members rejected scientific evidence supporting the influence of nutritional supplements, herbal products, dietary factors, pharmaceuticals, medical conditions or even environmental exposures on the risk of contracting Alzheimer's.

Now, just three months later, it turns out that there are big developments in the Alzheimer's fields—just not in new treatments. At a conference in Honolulu sponsored earlier this month by the National Institute on Aging and the Alzheimer's Disease Association, researchers from three working groups announced that by using new imaging technologies, genetic testing, and tests of blood and cerebrospinal fluid, it will soon be far easier to diagnose Alzheimer's—in some cases decades before symptoms have even appeared. These new tests are able to identify so-called biomarkers—amyloid plaques in the brain, genetic variants, proteins and other substances in body fluids—that signal a newly defined "pre-clinical" stage of Alzheimer's, when an individual has no symptoms but has positive biomarkers for the disease.

The chair of the working group charged with creating this pre-clinical definition was Reisa Sperling, assistant professor of neurology at Harvard Medical School. In a *MedScape* article, about the conference, Sperling said that the group struggled with the terminology for preclinical Alzheimer's disease (AD) and admitted that they knew it would provoke controversy. If these new tests for biomarkers—including a PET [positron-emission tomography] scan that can for the first time reveal amyloid plaques in a living brain—are used in the general public, it could double or triple the number of people diagnosed with Alzheimer's—at potentially great public and psychic expense.

But Sperling reminds critics that there are other medical conditions that are diagnosed before symptoms are apparent; including carcinoma in situ, asymptomatic coronary artery disease and kidney disease. What's important is that "not all individuals who have these risk factors or early stages of these other diseases ever go on to manifest symptoms." Still, the *MedScape* article adds, "treating high cholesterol has prevented many overt cardiac and stroke events."

Diagnosis of Alzheimer's Is Inexact

Currently, doctors diagnose Alzheimer's disease based on criteria developed 26 years ago; mainly by using neurological tests that track the progressive memory and

Technicians perform an experimental Alzheimer's blood test. New technologies in biomarker testing are making Alzheimer's easier to detect, sometimes far in advance of the actual appearance of symptoms. (© **Brian Bell/ Photo Researchers, Inc.**)

cognitive deficits that characterize the disease trajectory. A little over a decade ago, researchers began to recognize "mild cognitive impairment;" as a condition that is strongly linked with later development of full-blown Alzheimer's. They've also increasingly been using imaging techniques like MRIs and PET scans that reveal structural or functional changes in the brain associated with the disease. There is a gene variant, APOE4, which is also associated with AD: It occurs in about 40 percent of all people who develop late-onset AD and is present in about 25 to 30 percent of the general population. But AD dementia can only be definitively determined once a patient has died and an autopsy reveals the telltale amyloid plaques that are the hallmark of this disease.

It's been an inexact diagnostic practice. According to Gina Kolata, writing in *The New York Times* last month, "Even at the best medical centers, doctors often are wrong. Twenty percent of people with dementia—a loss of memory and intellectual functions—who received a diagnosis of Alzheimer's, did not have it. There was no plaque when their brains were biopsied. Half with milder memory loss, thought to be on their way to Alzheimer's, do not get the disease."

The goal of the new imaging techniques and other biomarker tests is to make diagnosis far less ambiguous. They would also help better identify risk factors (gene variants, environmental factors, etc.) that can be strong predictors of who gets AD. Finally, the tests would also greatly help in clinical research by identifying a larger pool of subjects who have an earlier stage of the disease to test whether promising drugs might prevent progression of AD. The initial emphasis, according to Creighton Phelps, director of the Alzheimer's Disease Center's program at

FAST FACT

According to the Alzheimer's Association, in the United States blacks are about twice as likely to have dementia as whites, and Hispanics are about one and a half times as likely to have it. This is thought to be due to increased risk factors in these groups rather than genetics.

the National Institute on Aging, will be on using these new tests in clinical research and validating the predictive value of the biomarkers.

But what happens when (as it inevitably will) diagnosis of pre-clinical Alzheimer's becomes more widely available? Dr. Ronald Pies, a professor of psychiatry at both SUNY Upstate Medical University and at Tufts University School of Medicine, writes in *Psychiatric Times*,

> The term "preclinical Alzheimer's Disease" may be adopted—but can "disease" as we ordinarily understand the term really be "pre-clinical"? And what will be the psychological effect of telling an asymptomatic patient, "You have preclinical Alzheimer's Disease"?

> Given that, at present, we have no treatments that can halt or reverse the progression of AD neuropathology, will we not create unnecessary anxiety in thousands of otherwise "normal" individuals, by carrying out widespread PET scanning for minor memory impairment? Furthermore, what if large-scale testing reveals that 20% or 40% of the general population over age 65 years have abnormal plaques on their PET scans? Will we be doing more harm than good by telling such individuals, as one expert suggested, "you are on the Alzheimer road"?

No Advantage to Early Testing

Nortin Hadler, writing in *The Healthcare Blog*, is more direct in stating the downside of pre-clinical testing for AD:

> There is a great public health danger in jumping the gun and prematurely using biomarkers in clinical practice for diagnosis or prognosis.

> [I]t offers no advantage to our patients today. Rather it is far more likely to engulf the patient in spurious inferences at great personal expense. Biomarkers have been tested only in small and highly selected groups of patients where they have impressive rates of false positive

Risk Factors for Alzheimer's Disease

Scientists do not know what causes Alzheimer's disease. Various risk factors have been proposed; however, according to a consensus statement by the National Institutes of Health, for many of them there is no scientific evidence of an association.

Associated with Increased Risk	No Consistent Association	Associated with Reduced Risk
ApoE gene variation	Obesity	Literacy
Diabetes	Hypertension	Social enrichment
Current smoking	Blood homocysteine level	Physical activity in later life
Depression	Cholinesterase inhibitors	Low-fat diet
Estrogen	Vitamins B12, C, and E	Light to moderate alcohol use
Nonsteroidal anti-inflammatory drugs	Gingko biloba; beta-carotene	

Taken from: National Institutes of Health, *Preventing Alzheimer's Disease and Cognitive Decline*, 2010. http://consensus.nih.gov/2010/alzstatement.htm.

results. That portends a great deal of over-diagnosis in less selected patients. Furthermore, all biomarker tests are expensive, some very expensive, and some have medical risks. None is near ready to be used in routine clinical practice.

Handler and Pies, along with others who are urging caution are right. Beyond financial planning and a jump on "putting affairs in order," there is little benefit to knowing you are going to get a degenerative and untreatable disease before you even have symptoms. Drug companies claim that they have plenty of promising AD drugs in their pipelines. But they have had scant success so far in developing effective Alzheimer's drugs—with some 30 failures occurring as far downstream as Phase 3 trials, according to a 2009 article in the journal *Current Alzheimer's Research*. "[A] formidable barrier to drug development is that we know very little about Alzheimer's disease, its pathogenesis, diagnosis, genetics and struggle with its clinical heterogeneity; we do not have full pre-clinical models on which to develop advanced therapeutic targets," according to the authors.

Here is where the new imaging techniques and other tests for biomarkers hold promise—in aiding in a deeper understanding of what actually causes Alzheimer's disease and as a method for identifying advanced therapeutic targets. But these tests must be used carefully only in research settings—well-designed, fully-considered and, ultimately, humane clinical trials. The technology is clearly not ready for public consumption.

Some Experts Believe Screening for Alzheimer's Disease Is Desirable

Marilynn Marchione

Doctors disagree about whether it is desirable to test people for Alzheimer's disease if they do not have significant symptoms or any symptoms at all. Many have brain plaques that may mean they will develop it, but some of them will not live long enough for that to happen, and even if it does, there are no good treatments. Nevertheless, some doctors believe that early testing is beneficial because it can lead people to avoid things that might make their condition worse, and it can give them access to drugs that treat symptoms, clinical trials of better drugs, and support services. Moreover, it enables them to plan for the future.

Marilynn Marchione is a medical writer for the Associated Press.

Picture yourself in Barbara Lesher's shoes: 54 years old and fearing you are developing Alzheimer's disease.

"I don't remember if I had a bath," said Lesher, who lives north of Harrisburg, Pa. "It took me two hours to follow a recipe. I drove to my childhood homestead the other week instead of my own home. It's really scary."

SOURCE: Marilynn Marchione, "Alzheimer's Debate: Test if You Can't Treat It?," *Yahoo! News*, July 21, 2011. Copyright © 2011 by the Associated Press. All rights reserved. Reproduced by permission.

Doctors are arguing about whether to test patients for signs of the incurable disease and tell them the results.

The debate raged this past week [June 2011] at the Alzheimer's Association International Conference in France, where research on new methods—easier brain scans, an eye test, a blood test—made it clear there soon may be more such tools available.

Here's why it's an issue: Many people have brain plaques, suggesting they might be developing Alzheimer's even if they don't have any symptoms. This plaque can be seen decades beforehand and does not ensure someone will get the disease. Many also won't live long enough to develop symptoms.

For those who do have Alzheimer's, there are no good treatments. Current drugs ease symptoms—they work for half who try them and for less than a year on average. Most experts think treatment starts too late, but there's no evidence that starting sooner or learning you have brain plaque will help. Experts are divided.

"We have to look for patients or signatures of the disease at earlier stages," urged Dr. Harald Hampel of the University of Frankfurt, Germany.

But Dr. Kenneth Rockwood of Dalhousie University in Halifax, Nova Scotia, Canada, says there is no data "to show that knowing makes any difference in outcomes. Until we do, this is going to be a tough sell."

More than 35 million people worldwide have Alzheimer's, the most common form of dementia. In the U.S., more than 5 million do—13 percent of those 65 and over, and 43 percent of those 85 and up, a rapidly growing group.

Diagnosed

Still, half of people who meet medical criteria for dementia have not been diagnosed with it, the Alzheimer's Association estimates. And many who are told they have Alzheimer's or are assumed to have it really don't.

Even when researchers use the best cognitive tests to enroll people in clinical trials, about 10 percent ultimately are discovered not to have the disease, said William Thies, the Alzheimer's Association's scientific director.

"The Alzheimer's drugs don't work in these folks, so there's no reason to expose them to those risks," said Thies, long an advocate of early diagnosis.

Misdiagnosis is a lost opportunity to help. A new medication or combination of medications may suddenly make someone appear demented. Brain fog can occur after surgery and abate over time. Sleep problems are common in older people and can cause profound confusion that can be misinterpreted as dementia, according to research presented at the conference by Dr. Kristine Yaffe of the University of California, San Francisco.

"Some of these are treatable" by avoiding naps during the day or treating sleep apnea, in which brief interruptions of breathing cause people to wake during the night, Yaffe said. Snoring is a big sign. Older people with sleep problems are more likely to be put in nursing homes, she said.

Methods of Screening for Alzheimer's Disease

Method of Screening	Cognitive Assessments	Genetic Testing	Biomarker Testing
In the doctor's office	✓	✓	Future
In research labs and clinical trials	✓	✓	✓
Test use and frequency	Commonly used, annual tests	Rarely used, onetime test	Rarely used, limited times

Taken from: http://silveradoblogs.com/news/diagnosing-alzheimer%E2%80%99s-review-of-currently-available-screening-methods/.

Dr. R. Scott Turner, director of the memory disorders program at Georgetown University Medical Center, has seen that all too often.

"I'm certainly in the camp that screening should be done," he said. Many patients are simply declared to have dementia without testing to see if they have another condition.

"Sometimes it's thyroid disease, or depression, or vitamin B-12 deficiency—something that's very treatable," he said.

Testing someone with symptoms is far less controversial than testing people with no symptoms but a lot of fear. Doctors worry that these newer methods, such as an easier type of brain scan that's expected to be available within months, will be directly marketed to the public, prompting expensive and excessive testing based on fear.

"The phrase you often hear is that the 'Big A' (Alzheimer's) has replaced the 'Big C' (cancer)" as a major source of fear, said Dr. Jason Karlawish, a University of Pennsylvania ethicist specializing in dementia issues.

> **FAST FACT**
>
> Most people with Alzheimer's disease have at least one other serious medical condition. Dementia makes management of these conditions more difficult and more expensive.

Recent guidelines by the U.S. National Institute on Aging and the Alzheimer's Association say these tests should be used only in research until they have been standardized and validated as useful and accurate tools.

A researcher using one of these tests, such as a spinal fluid check for a substance that may predict Alzheimer's risk, has no obligation to disclose the results to a patient until there is a meaningful treatment for the disease, Karlawish argued at the conference.

The more symptoms a patient has, the more justified it is to help understand what is known about possible reasons, he said.

Lynda Hogg of Edinburgh, Scotland, is very glad her doctors diagnosed her Alzheimer's in 2006. She is doing

At the Alzheimer's Association International Conference in France in June 2011, controversy raged over the value of new methods of brain scanning, eye testing, and blood testing for the disease. (© Horacio Villalobos/EPA/Landov)

exceptionally well on one of the existing drugs and is in a clinical trial for an experimental one she hopes will help her and help advance knowledge in the field.

At a discussion connected with the conference, she said the early diagnosis helped her get financial and legal matters in order and serve on the Scottish Dementia Working Group and the board of Alzheimer's Disease International.

"I am certain involvement keeps me focused and involved in society," she said.

The Alzheimer's Association says early diagnosis and evaluation can bring the following benefits:

- Treatment of reversible causes of impairment.
- Access to drugs that help treat symptoms.
- Inclusion in clinical trials that give expert care.
- Avoiding drugs that can worsen cognition.
- Letting others know of a need for help managing medicines and daily life.

• Easing anxiety about the cause of symptoms.
• Access to education, training and support services.
• The ability to plan for the future.

Lesher, the woman from Pennsylvania, wishes she had a clearer picture of what lies ahead for her.

"Not being able to get diagnosed is the most frustrating thing in the world," she said.

Language Skills in Youth May Reduce Risk of Alzheimer's Disease in Old Age

Amanda Gardner

According to analysis of essays written by women when they were young, those who have greater-than-average language skills in youth are less likely to have Alzheimer's disease in old age. This is true even if their brains, when examined during autopsy, contain the plaques characteristic of the disease, possibly because these brains contain larger neurons that may compensate. The data come from an ongoing study of Catholic nuns who donated their brains after death. They had written essays when they entered the convent in their late teens or early twenties that were preserved in the convent's archives. Researchers do not know how language skills protected them from the effects of brain pathology, but they suspect that people have a cognitive reserve that is increased by mental activity early in life.

Amanda Gardner is a reporter for HealthDay, a health news service.

SOURCE: Amanda Gardner, "Greater Language Skills in 20s May Guard Against Alzheimer's," HealthDay, July 8, 2009. http://www .healthday.com. Copyright © 2009 by HealthDay. All rights reserved. Reproduced by permission.

Women with greater language abilities in early adulthood were less likely to have Alzheimer's disease later in life, even when autopsies revealed the clear brain changes that are hallmarks of the disease.

Also, the brains of women without symptoms of Alzheimer's housed bigger neurons, according to a study appearing in the July 9 [2009] online edition of *Neurology*.

"We noticed that the neurons in this group of people are larger and we also know that the same group of people we call asymptomatic also had higher language skills during their 20s," said study author Dr. Diego Iacono, a research fellow in neuropathology at Johns Hopkins University in Baltimore.

It's possible that the larger neurons compensated for the brain plaques and tangles that are usually indicative of Alzheimer's, the authors stated.

An analysis of the brains of thirty-eight nuns reached the conclusion that young girls with greater than average language skills are less likely to have Alzheimer's disease in old age.
(© Urbanmyth/Alamy)

The findings could also mean that language abilities in the early 20s can predict the risk of developing dementia several decades later.

A previous study, this one in men, also found larger neurons in individuals who had plaques and tangles but no clinical evidence of Alzheimer's.

For the current study, researchers examined the brains of 38 deceased Catholic nuns, part of the ongoing Nun Study.

Women were divided into two groups: those with symptoms of memory loss along with plaques and tangles and those with no memory loss whether or not they had plaques or tangles.

Language Skills May Protect Against Alzheimer's

Essays written by the women when they first entered the convent in their late teens or early 20s were analyzed for richness of language skills, including how many ideas were expressed per 10 words, number of verbs and adjectives in one sentence and more.

Women without memory problems scored 20 percent higher on language tests (though not grammar tests) than did women with memory issues. "We think this percentage could be higher if we could increase the sample size of the subjects to examine. We are working on that," Iacono said.

"The novelty is that these people were normal [cognitively] but they have Alzheimer's disease pathology like the people with dementia," Iacono said. "It's amazing that, even though you have a certain amount of pathology in your brain, you are not demented. You have some protective mechanism."

It's not clear whether that protection comes from genetic factors or from more studying during the first two

FAST FACT

Studies have found that people who in early and midlife have had mind-challenging hobbies such as reading, working jigsaw puzzles, and playing games are much less likely to develop dementia than those who have spent their time watching television.

The Effect of Education on Risk of Dementia

Studies have shown that people with more education have less risk of developing dementia in old age. Researchers examined test data from people who had donated their brains and found that although education made no difference in whether or not they had neurodegenerative brain damage by the time they died, it did make the damage less likely to result in dementia.

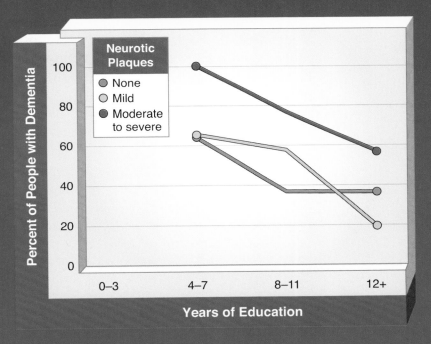

Taken from: C. Brayne et al., "Education, the Brain and Dementia: Neuroprotection or Compensation?," *Brain*, June 6, 2010. www.eclipsestudy.eu/pages/publications/Brain_2010.pdf.

decades of life, although it does fit with the "cognitive reserve" theory.

"The idea is that we have a sort of cognitive reserve that we start to increase during our second and third decades of life, and you can spend this reserve when you get older," Iacono explained. "In this way, you can avoid the manifestation of dementia even if you have some pathology. This is something we didn't expect."

"This is the second independent sample with the same result. We're back to the metaphor of the brain as a computer and a muscle," said Dr. Gary J. Kennedy, director of geriatric psychiatry at Montefiore Medical Center in New York City. "In volunteers who had no signs of Alzheimer's but did have the plaques and tangles, the neurons were actually larger and more functional with more connections."

The paper also showed an increased risk for cognitive impairment in people with the APOE4 gene and a protective effect in those with the APOE2 gene.

The authors are now investigating to see if they can show a connection between the language skills and these particular genes.

Antipsychotic Drugs Have Severe Side Effects and Should Rarely Be Given to Dementia Patients

Harvard Medical School

Antipsychotic drugs are intended for treatment of people with mental illnesses such as schizophrenia and bipolar disorder. However, they are also often used on elderly people with dementia whose behavior is disruptive, in spite of the fact that the US Food and Drug Administration has issued warnings against this. Since 1987 the law has stated that nursing home residents cannot be given antipsychotic drugs merely for the convenience of the staff, but it happens anyway. Although these drugs may help some dementia patients, there is no strong evidence that they do, and they often have serious side effects. A review of controlled studies showed that patients who were taking them had up to a 50 percent higher death rate than those who were not. Nevertheless, some doctors believe that these drugs are needed in the case of patients who are agitated and aggressive.

SOURCE: "Antipsychotic Drugs in Dementia." Excerpted from the Harvard Mental Health Newsletter, August 2007, pp. 4–5. Copyright © 2007, Harvard University. For more information visit: http://www.health.harvard.edu.

Antipsychotic drugs are officially approved mainly for the treatment of schizophrenia and bipolar disorder, but they are also used for many other purposes, and one of the most controversial is reducing disruptive behavior among elderly people with dementia. In the last few years the FDA [US Food and Drug Administration] has required new warnings for drug labels, and controlled studies continue to raise questions about the risks and benefits of a practice that is still common.

Concern about this issue is not new. A federal law passed in 1987 provides that residents of nursing homes and assisted-living facilities receiving government financial support cannot be given antipsychotic drugs merely because they are wandering, insomniac, or uncooperative—that is, because staff members are inconvenienced. The drugs should be used only for agitated, aggressive, or psychotic behavior that is either distressing to the patients themselves or dangerous to others. Clinicians who prescribe the drugs must document the diagnosis and their reasons for the prescription and record all side effects.

The guidelines have not prevented continued heavy use of antipsychotic drugs in institutions for the elderly. One review of the records of 2.5 million nursing home residents found that 28% of them had received at least one prescription for an antipsychotic drug during the years 2000 and 2001. And the question is still being raised whether the drugs are prescribed inappropriately or at doses that are too high.

There is some evidence that the drugs can be effective. A review of 16 controlled studies by the Cochrane Collaboration found that the second-generation or atypical antipsychotics risperidone (Risperdal), olanzapine (Zyprexa), and aripiprazole (Abilify) might reduce agitation, aggression, and psychosis in patients with demen-

FAST FACT

According to an investigation by the *Boston Globe,* in 2010 at least one-quarter of the residents of 21 percent of US nursing homes received antipsychotic medications when they did not have illnesses for which these medications are recommended.

tia, although there was little evidence about the merit of long-term use.

Findings from observational studies are sometimes encouraging. A recent two-year study in Finland, for example, found that nursing home patients with dementia who did not use antipsychotic drugs were more likely to be admitted to hospitals and more likely to die than those taking second-generation antipsychotics.

But that study was not a randomized controlled trial, which is the strongest form of evidence. Recent findings from controlled trials suggest skepticism about the value of antipsychotic drugs in dementia, especially where

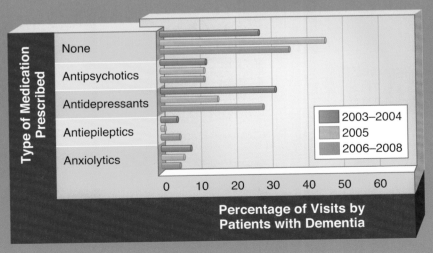

The Effect of Warning Against Antipsychotic Drugs on Prescriptions to Dementia Patients

In 2005 the FDA issued a warning against inappropriate prescription of antipsychotic drugs to dementia patients. This resulted in a slight decline in their use and no evidence that other psychotropic drugs were substituted for them.

Type of Medication Prescribed:
- None
- Antipsychotics
- Antidepressants
- Antiepileptics
- Anxiolytics

Percentage of Visits by Patients with Dementia: 0, 10, 20, 30, 40, 50, 60

Legend: 2003–2004, 2005, 2006–2008

Taken from: Vibha C.A. Desai et al. "Impact of the Food and Drug Administration's Antipsychotic Black Box Warning on Psychotropic Drug Prescribing in Elderly Patients with Dementia in Outpatient and Office-Based Settings." *Alzheimer's and Dementia*, January 2012. www.sciencedirect.com/science/article/pii/S1552526011027178.

long-term use is concerned. In a 2004 study, for example, withdrawing 100 people with dementia from antipsychotic drugs had no effect on their behavior, psychiatric symptoms, or quality of life.

The most thorough controlled study was the National Institutes of Mental Health–sponsored Clinical Antipsychotic Trials of Intervention Effectiveness—Alzheimer's Disease (CATIE-AD). More than 400 patients with dementia living at home or in assisted-living facilities (but not in nursing homes) were divided into four groups and treated for eight months with either risperidone, olanzapine, quetiapine (Seroquel), or a placebo. Results were similar in all four groups. About 80% of the patients stopped taking medications before the trial ended because of ineffectiveness or side effects.

The Cochrane Collaboration study found that the antipsychotic drug olanzapine, brand name Zyprexa, and others might reduce agitation, aggression, and psychosis in patients with dementia. (© **AP Images/Darron Cummings**)

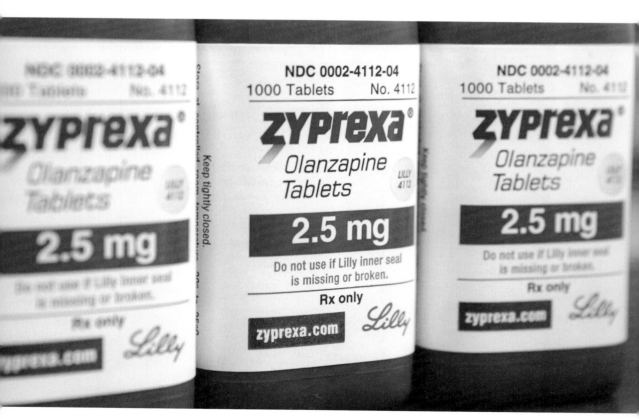

Risks Outweigh Benefits

A 2007 report covering 84 studies issued by the Agency for Healthcare Research and Quality, part of the Department of Health and Human Services, concluded that there is little evidence to support the use of second-generation antipsychotic drugs by elderly people with dementia.

Antipsychotic drugs help some patients, but for many the risks will outweigh the benefits. The side effects, which are more common and severe in the elderly, include tremors, drowsiness, and weight gain. In the CATIE-AD trial, patients taking the drugs gained an average of one-half to one pound per month, depending on the drug; those taking the placebo lost an average of one pound per month. Antipsychotic drugs may raise the risk of high cholesterol, diabetes, and heart arrhythmias. There is even some speculation that their anticholinergic properties reduce the effect of the cholinesterase inhibitors that are used to slow cognitive decline in dementia.

In April 2005, the FDA required a Black Box warning on prescription labels for antipsychotic drugs. The order was based on a review of 17 controlled studies in which patients taking the drugs had up to a 50% higher death rate than those taking a placebo, mostly from cardiovascular disease and pneumonia.

Despite the disappointing findings, clinicians have not given up on the use of antipsychotic drugs for problems associated with dementia. The American Association for Geriatric Psychiatry responded to the CATIE-AD study by urging federal regulatory agencies not to "prevent physicians from exercising clinical judgment." Its statement points out that many patients, especially those living in nursing homes, have more severe symptoms than the study participants.

Even the lead investigator of the CATIE-AD study has said that he still prescribes antipsychotic drugs—for short-term use only—in patients who are psychotic, agitated, or aggressive and do not respond to other measures. If drug use is necessary, experts recommend starting at a low dose and gradually increasing it. The need for continuing the drug should be evaluated after three to six months. Clinicians are advised to document their reasons for prescribing the drug and their understanding of the risk-benefit ratio. They should periodically check the patient's cardiopulmonary and cerebrovascular health, and involved family members should be included in discussions about the risks and benefits.

Implanted Microchips Do Not Benefit Alzheimer's Patients, and Unapproved Trials Are Unethical

Penn Bullock

In 2007 identifying microchips (commonly known as VeriChips, the brand name under which they were originally marketed) were injected into two hundred Florida Alzheimer's patients, ostensibly as part of a harmless project. The nursing home from which these patients came claimed that this would be useful for identifying them if they became lost, as people with dementia sometimes do. However, doctors have since declared that the "project" was actually a research study on human subjects and was both unethical and illegal because it had not been approved by an institutional review board. There were health risks involved of which participants had not been informed, and many dementia patients are incapable of giving informed consent in any case. Furthermore, ethicists point out that identifying lost Alzheimer's patients is rarely a problem; usually the need is to find them.

Penn Bullock is a Florida-based investigative journalist who has written for many national publications.

SOURCE: Penn Bullock, "Under Your Skin," James Randi Educational Foundation, March 17, 2010. http://www.randi.org. Copyright © 2010 by Penn Bullock. All rights reserved. Reproduced by permission.

In 2007, the PositiveID Corporation in Florida injected microchips into Alzheimer's patients as part of what it termed a "two-year study." Up to 200 test subjects, many incapacitated, were supplied by a nursing home in West Palm Beach called Alzheimer's Community Care [ACC], which PositiveID has sponsored at fundraisers.

Today, based on new information, doctors allege the study violated medical ethics and regulatory law. PositiveID appears to have abused science for profit, banking on public and even professional ignorance of medical ethics.

PositiveID, known as VeriChip at the time of the study, markets the world's first human-implantable microchip, approved by the FDA [US Food and Drug Administration] for medical use in 2004. (In 2005, former Secretary of Health and Human Services Tommy Thompson resigned from government and joined the company's board.) The rice-grain sized device is stuck into the flesh with a nearly foot-long syringe. It contains a serial number that can be read by a scanner and then matched with a person's online medical profile in an emergency.

PositiveID and Alzheimer's Community Care claimed Alzheimer's patients were in special need of implantation. The CEO of the ACC, Mary Barnes, told *USA Today* that the chip "could be invaluable in identifying lost patients—for instance, if a hurricane strikes Florida." But Dr. Robin Fiore, a professor of ethics at Florida Atlantic University [FAU] and a national lecturer on medicine, said Barnes' claim amounts to pseudo-science. Usually, the difficulty is in finding missing Alzheimer's patients, not identifying them. "This is not going to find lost people," she said, noting that PositiveID's chips are not GPS-equipped [containing a Global Positioning System device]. "And if [the patients' caregivers] think this will help them find their lost loves ones, they're just confused. They've just been misinformed." Mrs. Barnes also told *USA Today* that "both the patients and their legal guardians must consent to the implants before receiving them." To the contrary, PositiveID admits that many patients were unable to give informed consent, so their legal guardians enrolled them.

On his Fox News show last October [2009], Glenn Beck reinforced the idea that the chip is a big help to Alzheimer's patients, while dispelling conspiracy theories about the company. "They have fantastic technology if you're an Alzheimer's patient," he assured. But "it's very, very bad if, say, former leader of Nazi Germany, Adolf] Hitler has this technology." He urged his viewers to be skeptical. "You must stay vigilant, be aware, watch for it. . . . I know the times we're living in. Vigilance is the key word." If Glenn Beck had not merely repeated the word "vigilance" and instead approached the company as a skeptic, he would have discovered that the experiment on Alzheimer's patients lacked standard scientific oversight.

Study Was Not Approved

As PositiveID spokeswoman Allison Tomek now admits, no Institutional Review Board (IRB) ever approved the study, which ended in 2009. IRBs are integral to sound medical science. As panels of experts and laymen, they're supposed to authorize and oversee all studies on humans in order to guard against abuse and protect subjects' rights. According to four experts, PositiveID's study would've required an IRB under federal regulations.

In a phone interview, Mrs. Tomek offered an excuse for not getting one. She insisted the Alzheimer's initiative was a "project, not a study." In an email, she explained: ". . . Our relationship with Alzheimer's Community Care to provide their patients and caregivers with the microchip . . . was not a research study or experiment, so IRB review is not required."

Her claim is belied by a company press release in which PositiveID CEO Scott Silverman explicitly called the initiative a study. "We are extremely pleased to partner with Alzheimer's Community Care on this relevant study," he said. And, in filings to the SEC [Securities and Exchange Commission], PositiveID again called it a "two-year, 200 patient study." The filing states: "We believe that if the results of these and other clinical studies . . . are sufficiently compelling, the Center for Medicare and Medicaid Services may determine that the [VeriChip] Health Link microchip . . . is reimbursable under Medicare and Medicaid." The transformation of the "study" into a "project" seems to be a recent semantic development.

Reached by phone, the CEO of Alzheimer's Community Care, Mary Barnes, repeated the mantra that it was a so-called project. "We did participate in a project with [PositiveID]," she said, pausing dramatically. "A *project*. We had legal documents reviewed by counsel. The project was for the benefit of patients and caregivers. . . ." When asked if the ACC had gotten an IRB, she abruptly hung up the phone.

"Whether you call it a project or a study is irrelevant," said Dr. Robin Fiore, the FAU professor. "You could call it Fred. It's obviously human subjects research."

Unethical and Perhaps Illegal

Dr. Kenneth Goodman, head of the University of Miami's Bioethics Program, said of the study: "Any research that does not include an IRB does not meet the ethical standard."

PositiveID's study may have violated more than just a universal ethical standard for research. Dr. Deborah Peel, a practicing physician and founder of two national organizations on patient privacy, said in a phone interview that she thought the study "probably violates federal law."

FAU professor Dr. Fiore agreed: "The problem here is failure to conform to regulations governing research," Dr. Fiore said. "So it's a regulatory violation subject to fines." She confirmed PositiveID could even lose its FDA approval for the microchip. "It's possible. That's pretty nuclear, so the violation would have to be egregious."

And a CDC [Centers for Disease Control and Prevention] official in charge of regulating human research, who asked to remain anonymous, concurred, calling the study a "slam-dunk regulatory violation." He elaborated in an email: "To conduct [a study] without independent review is not right—it may place people who have volunteered their time at risk. . . . In terms of regulation, the device is not approved for this use, it falls under FDA regulation, and it requires independent review by an IRB."

FDA press spokeswoman Karen Riley said by phone that she had asked the FDA's own ethicists whether the study required an IRB. The answer she got was yes. "The bottom line is you would need an IRB because it's a trial of a medical device," she said. Another FDA spokesman,

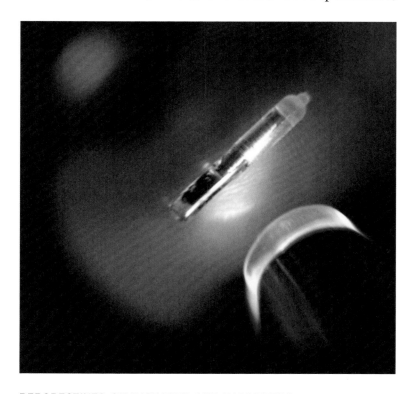

The implanting of the VeriChip into two hundred Florida Alzheimer's patients in 2007 was considered unethical and illegal by many medical professionals. (© Colin Brawley/Reuters/Landov)

Dick Thompson, confirmed the study wouldn't have been ethical without an IRB, but left the legal question open. In an email, he said: "We can't make a determination about this particular study based on the information we have in hand." But, he said: "In general, we believe an IRB or its equivalent is ethically appropriate—if not required—for any study involving a human population, especially a population of vulnerable people such as those with Alzheimer's disease."

Implantation May Have Health Risks

Dr. Fiore articulated the risks of doing the study on Alzheimer's patients. "There's the question about implanting something in a person that may have health risks for frail people: their skin doesn't heal as well and they're much more subject to infections." Alluding to reports in the *Associated Press* from 2005 that the chips caused tumors in mice, she also said: "It's important to note that their [2004] FDA approval came before the information about the potential cancer risks occurred. . . . The question of whether those are reasonable risks to express to people is part of what the IRB would have to decide. Without an IRB, I'm guessing they would never be mentioned."

It's also doubtful whether PositiveID let test subjects know that the chip, according to its own manual, could malfunction in ambulances and around MRIs and X-ray machines due to radio interference. That would call into question the chip's very purpose as a means of pulling up a person's medical information in ambulances and hospitals.

What makes PositiveID's alleged regulatory violation especially worrying is that the company announced last December [2009] it will be conducting a study on people with diabetes in Florida. Asked

> ## FAST FACT
>
> The VeriChip met strong opposition from privacy advocates, who argued that, when combined with GPS technology, it could be used to track people and might become compulsory for everyone. It was taken off the American market in 2010 but has been acquired by another company and sold elsewhere.

Risk Factors for Wandering in Patients with Dementia

People with dementia are apt to go out by themselves without telling anyone, sometimes during the night, and become confused as to who or where they are. This is known as "wandering."

Risk Factors for Wandering in Patients with Dementia
Unfamiliar environment
Recent medication change
Being left alone
Changes in routine
Disoriented to familiar surroundings
Expressed desire to "go home" or to a place often visited in the past

Taken from: P.E. Lester, A. Garite, and I. Kohen. "Wandering and Elopement in Nursing Homes." *Annals of Long-Term Care: Clinical Care and Aging*, 2012;20(3):32–36.

if there would be an IRB for that study, the company's spokeswoman, Mrs. Tomek, said there "might or might not, depending on the elements in the study." Meanwhile, Alzheimer's Community Care, whose CEO hung up the phone rather than disclose whether her organization consulted an IRB, has been nominated for the 2010 "Best Practices Award" for non-profits by Palm Beach County's Clerk and Comptroller.

Capping off the irony, this June the ACC and PositiveID will launch the 2010 Alzheimer's Educational Conference, attracting speakers from across the United States to "educate family caregivers and healthcare professionals about the latest research and standards of care for those with Alzheimer's." Given the accusation that the ACC and PositiveID flouted FDA regulations, those companies may be the ones most in need of an education.

High Doses of Aricept Do Not Benefit Alzheimer's Patients and Should Not Have Been Approved

Patrick Malone

Drugs for Alzheimer's disease are of such moderate benefit that doctors cannot always tell whether they have helped a patient or whether symptoms would have temporarily lessened without them. When the patent on a leading drug called Aricept was about to expire, its manufacturer got the US Food and Drug Administration (FDA) to approve a higher-dose pill that it claimed worked better, a strategy that allowed the company to keep selling the brand-name drug with less competition from generic versions than the standard-dose pills. However, according to an article by experts published in a medical journal, the higher dose results in no significant improvement in patients yet has much worse side effects. The FDA should not have approved it, they said, and in doing so the agency was either incompetent or corrupt.

Patrick Malone is a patient safety advocate and attorney who represents seriously injured people in medical malpractice and product liability lawsuits. He is a former investigative journalist and the author or coauthor of several books.

SOURCE: Patrick Malone, "Aricept 23—A Misleading Drug Enabled by the FDA," Technorati.com, March 31, 2012. Copyright © 2012 by Patrick Malone. All rights reserved. Reproduced by permission.

In some ways, Alzheimer's is like arthritis. Its symptoms can wax and wane, making it difficult to determine if a particular treatment is successful. Who's to say if a symptom subsided because a drug worked, or because it was going to diminish anyway?

And, like arthritis, Alzheimer's cannot be cured, only moderated. That can lead sufferers and the people who care for them to become desperate for any new treatment—what have they got to lose?

So dementia leaves its victims particularly vulnerable to new, if not improved, ways to treat it, and one such recent attempt raised the ire of two professors at Dartmouth's Institute for Health Policy and Clinical Practice. As reported by Merrill Goozner, Drs. Lisa Schwartz and Steven Woloshin claim that the FDA [US Food and Drug Administration] has "breached [its] own regulatory standard" in approving a new dosage of a best-selling Alzheimer's drug.

Aricept, whose generic name is donepezil, is earning its manufacturers $2 billion a year for improving memory lapses in the short term. With its patent about to expire (Aricept was introduced in 1996), and generic manufacturers poised to compete with their own versions, manufacturers Eisai and Pfizer were motivated to keep the cash flowing. They appealed to the FDA to approve a higher dosage, claiming that a trial of 1,400 patients demonstrated improvements in the ability to think. The feds gave the drug makers three more years to market the stronger drug exclusively.

But as Schwartz and Woloshin wrote in the *British Medical Journal* (*BMJ*), patients had only slightly better cognition on the higher dose, and it had absolutely no effect on day-to-day functioning, the measure by which caregivers determine disease status. Unfortunately, the stronger Aricept conferred significantly negative side

FAST FACT

Five drugs have been approved for Alzheimer's disease, but they are effective in slowing its progression for merely six to twelve months on average, and only for about half the individuals who take them.

effects, including nausea and vomiting. For patients with dementia, that can lead to pneumonia. The FDA had told the trial sponsors that the drug wouldn't be approved unless it had a positive impact that patient caregivers could notice.

So at best, the contrary approval makes the FDA look dysfunctional; at worst, it looks incompetent and corrupt.

Untrue Claims

Aricept's manufacturers went merrily along their marketing way, their advertisements implying to consumers that the drug helped the Alzheimer brain function better, but not mentioning the severity of side effects. And the ads aimed at doctors, Schwartz and Woloshin charged, were worse: "[They contain] a stunningly erroneous statement in a large bold font: 'Patients on Aricept 23 mg/day experienced important clinical benefit on both measures [cognition and overall functioning],' which is simply not true. In fact, this statement is directly contradicted by a statement in a smaller plain font that says that the results for global function 'did not show statistical significance.'"

That doctors are considered easy marks for Big Pharma is depressingly old news.

Unless drug company labels make inaccurate claims, the FDA does not intervene, even if a drug's risks, benefits and uncertainties aren't communicated.

As explained in the *Los Angeles Times*, drug companies commonly respond to an expiring patent with a practice called "evergreening." To prolong the profitability of successful drugs, they make a slight change to a drug's formula or dosage, or combine it with another drug. These are legal measures that require FDA approval.

Aricept's new 23-milligram tablet, the *Times* story explained, "created a dose that couldn't be reproduced by any combination of Aricept's existing 5- and 10-milligram pills, making the product new enough to win a three-year reprieve from low-cost competitors."

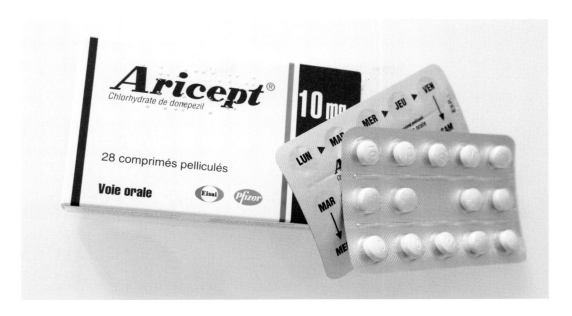

Professors at Dartmouth's Institute for Health Policy and Clinical Practice claim that in approving larger doses of the drug Aricept, the FDA breached its own regulatory standards. (© **BSIP/UIG Via Getty Images**)

Dr. Howard Brody, a medical ethicist at the University of Texas Medical Branch in Galveston, told the *Times* that the Aricept 23 case is "a perfect storm" of commercial marketing and regulatory failure whose victims are patients who are desperate, discouraged and vulnerable.

As Dr. Marcia Angell, former editor of the *New England Journal of Medicine*, told the newspaper, Big Pharma's manipulative ads illustrate "very well how drug companies exaggerate the benefits of their drugs, minimize the side effects and through misleading marketing to both doctors and the public convince them that a new version of a drug, with a new patent, is better than the old one, whose patent has expired."

If your loved one is prescribed Aricept for his or her Alzheimer's disease, ask the doctor what is the dose. If it's 23 milligrams, ask for a lower dosage. It's just that simple.

Prescribing Unproven Drugs for Alzheimer's Disease Would Be Unethical

Katie Moisse

Scientists test drugs on animals long before the drugs are ready for human trials—often new drugs, but sometimes ones that are already approved for different purposes. Once a drug has been approved, physicians can legally prescribe it for any illness they feel it will help. So when families of Alzheimer's patients learned that bexarotene, a drug for skin cancer, has been found to clear the amyloid plaques characteristic of Alzheimer's disease from the brains of mice, they wanted their doctors to let them try it. They felt that their loved ones' condition was so bad that they had nothing to lose and that they did not have time to wait until human testing was done. But physicians do not believe that would be ethical. Drugs that work on mice often have no effect on humans—or else prove toxic. Moreover, insurance companies do not cover experimental treatment, and bexarotene would cost up to twenty-five hundred dollars per day. Some families feel the possibility of benefit would be worth the risk, but most doctors disagree.

Katie Moisse is a health reporter for ABC News.

SOURCE: Katie Moisse, "Alzheimer's Disease: Drug Sparks Hope, Desperation," *ABC News*, February 14, 2012. Copyright © 2012 by ABC News. All rights reserved. Reproduced by permission.

John Vasse would do anything to save his wife, June, from Alzheimer's—the degenerative disease that's swiftly stealing her memory.

It's been three years since the devastating diagnosis [in 2009], and Vasse knows the disease will progress and eventually kill his wife of 42 years. So when he heard last week that a skin cancer drug had reversed Alzheimer's symptoms in mice, he was determined to get hold of it.

"What's the harm in trying?" said Vasse, 68, who lives with 66-year-old June in St. Louis. "If someone doesn't know who they are and needs to be cleaned and toileted several times daily, what could possibly be worse than that?"

Investigational drugs are considered experimental treatment by insurance companies and are not covered. Such treatment can cost up to twenty-five hundred dollars per day. (© AP Images/Seth Wenig)

The drug, bexarotene, whose trade name is Targretin, quickly cleared abnormal plaques of a protein called beta amyloid from the brain and improved memory in three different mouse models of Alzheimer's disease, according to a study published Thursday [February 15, 2012] in the journal *Science*. Beta amyloid is just one feature of Alzheimer's disease in humans.

Because bexarotene is already approved by the U.S. Food and Drug Administration [FDA] for skin cancer, doctors can legally prescribe it "off-label" for other conditions. But Alzheimer's experts urge families to temper their hope until the drug is proved safe and effective by years of clinical trials—a tall order for the country's 5.4 million patients and 14.9 million caregivers.

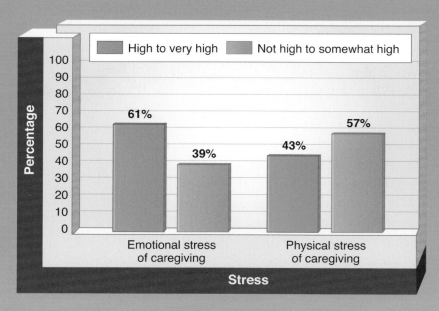

Taken from: Carissa Rogers. "Unpaid Alzheimer and Dementia Caregivers Provide $202.6 Billion in Service." Technorati, March 15, 2011. http://technorati.com/women/article/unpaid-alzheimer-and-dementia-caregivers-provide/.

"At this point in time, it would really be unethical for a physician to prescribe the medication and, I think, foolish for the patient to take it," said William Thies, chief medical and scientific officer for the Alzheimer's Association.

Serious Side Effects

Like other cancer drugs, bexarotene can produce serious side effects, including headaches, hair loss, nausea and depression, and can increase cholesterol levels, according to the National Institutes of Health. In elderly Alzheimer's patients, many of whom take multiple medications, bexarotene could interact and interfere with other drugs.

Thies said the Alzheimer's Association received more than a dozen calls about bexarotene after the *Science* study was published last week. Other doctors contacted by ABC News said they, too, had been contacted by caregivers clamoring for the drug.

"I just said we don't know if it's safe or effective," said Dr. George Grossberg, director of geriatric psychiatry at St. Louis University, who treats June Vasse. "I don't think we should be prescribing medications if we have no idea how to use them. It's irresponsible."

The list of drugs that have been promising in mouse models of Alzheimer's but disappointing in humans is long. Some have been too toxic, while others have failed to outperform a sugar pill. The last drug approved by the FDA for Alzheimer's disease was memantine in 2003. And for patients and their families, the string of negative trials has taken its toll.

"People are thinking, 'Look. I might not be around in two or three years to benefit from the next clinical trial,'" said Dr. Ronald Petersen, director of the Alzheimer's

> **FAST FACT**
>
> According to the Alzheimer's Association, more than 15 million Americans, mostly family members or other relatives, are unpaid caregivers for a person with dementia. In 2011 they provided an estimated 17.4 billion hours of home care, valued at over $210 billion.

Disease Research Center at the Mayo Clinic in Rochester, Minn. "I certainly empathize with them. But on the medical side, we certainly can't recommend a drug that has only been shown to have some possible benefits in a mouse model."

High Cost

Beyond safety and efficacy, there's the cost. Because bexarotene is not an approved Alzheimer's treatment, insurance companies won't cover it.

"The drug will cost between $1,200 and $2,500 per day out of pocket," said Dr. Sam Gandy, director of the Mount Sinai Center for Cognitive Health in New York. Gandy said families who said they have "nothing to lose" could risk money and "unexpected side effects of a dangerous treatment, and loss of the loved one rather than the gradual deterioration from the disease."

For Vasse, who said he has been "paralyzed" by depression and anxiety since his wife started to slip away, the prospect of bringing her back is almost worth the risk. He has agreed to wait until Grossberg, her doctor, gives the go-ahead, and said he'd be willing to pay for the drug out of pocket. But, "of course, I'd be burning up money we might need for assisted living," he said. "It's a decision we caregivers must make."

CHAPTER 3

Personal Narratives

A High School Student's Prize-Winning Recollection of Her Alzheimer's-Stricken Grandmother

Olivia L. Vehslage

Olivia L. Vehslage, a high school student in Wethersfield, Connecticut, won a college scholarship in the 2012 completion sponsored by the Alzheimer's Foundation of America for the following essay, titled "Recollection Roulette." In it she tells about her memories of her grandmother as she was before she got Alzheimer's disease and how hard it is to see her as she is now. Vehslage's grandmother is not usually able to recognize people and is often confused about time and place. But she is still much more than the weakness of her mind reveals, and her legacy of strength will live on after she is gone.

Photo on previous page. Caring for a loved one with dementia can be difficult both emotionally and financially, but it can be rewarding, too. (© Tips Images/Tips Italia Srl a socio unico/Alamy)

SOURCE: Olivia L. Vehslage, "Recollection Roulette," Alzheimer's Foundation of America, 2012. This essay was originally written as a submission for the 2012 Alzheimer's Foundation of America (AFA) Teens College Scholarship Contest. The author received the second runner-up award. Reprinted with permission from the Alzheimer's Foundation of America. Visit AFA Teens (www.afateens.org), an award-winning AFA division that seeks to raise awareness about Alzheimer's disease and engage young people in the cause, for more information and resources.

I could see it in my grandmother's eyes before she even said a word. All I had to do was watch her focus in on me as I leaned over her wheelchair to give her a hug, and I knew she knew me. It was a minor victory in a battle she's rapidly losing, but it was knowledge I treasured nonetheless. I was determined to hold up my end of the bargain, saving each word in a corner of my mind, for if she could remember to say my name, I could remember she had. Sitting in a chair across from her, I drank in her struggle, wrinkles fighting laugh lines, powder blush against pale skin, bright blue combating cataracts.

Suddenly, my grandmother pointed at a picture of a six-year-old me resting on the nearby coffee table and remarked in her honeyed southern drawl, "Sweetie, do you see that?"

Studying my younger self, I grinned and nodded.

"That's my granddaughter," Nana chatted away breezily. "She lives in Connecticut. She must be . . . well, I've plumb forgotten how old she'd be now!"

My smile froze, slipped off and shattered on the floor. I swallowed hard and felt my hands begin to shake, a nervous tic of my grandmother's that was passed down to my father and now to me.

The Grandmother I Remember

I never knew either of my grandfathers; both died well before I was born. Growing up, I idolized my Nana Ruth, a shining example of the steadfast, capable, self-sufficient woman I wish to become. Her first house, the one my father grew up in, lay on the edge of a golf course in the peaceful suburbs of Wilmington, Delaware. As a child, my father, mother, brother and I would make the six-hour drive from Connecticut to visit her at least four or five times a year. She would be standing in the driveway to meet us, always wearing coke bottle glasses and an ankle length dress with a hideous floral print straight out of the 60s. Having lived in the South most of her life, Nana

Ruth's thick accent has never tempered despite raising her family in the North where she's the only one who says "y'all" and drinks iced tea so sweet a single sip makes your teeth hurt.

There was no exact moment I discovered my grandmother had Alzheimer's disease. It seemed an impossible occurrence that this amazingly adept woman could ever be unable to fend for herself. Gradually, not remembering where she placed her glasses became not remembering where her house was, which became not always remembering my name. As she reached 80, she moved from her home in the suburbs to an assisted living facility where nurses came to bring her to dinner and to provide medication when needed. My birthday gifts from Nana Ruth used to be highly anticipated; she always knew exactly what to get and her cards would make me giggle. Now, my gift from her is really from my father, who buys a present in her name since she doesn't recall when my birthday is. The lack of a card in her delicate penmanship just affirmed the reality that had been slowly dawning in my mind, that my grandmother wasn't the same anymore. The concept seemed absurd, but as the years went on it became more and more like a joke that only I was laughing at.

The image of my grandmother in her driveway is how I like to remember her—the Nana Ruth I hold onto in my memories. I try to pretend that there isn't a distinction between the strong woman I once knew and the shadow that sits in her wheelchair staring into space, but it's futile. When I wheel her into the bathroom to redo her makeup and she pulls out a blue ballpoint pen to draw on her eyebrows, I know it isn't her. When she paints on a coral red smile that looks clownish against her pale skin, I know it isn't her. Then she looks up at me, the finished product, and I know that if this were a stranger I saw with blue eyebrows, scarlet lips and too bright blush, I would probably laugh a little. But it isn't a stranger, it's my grandmother, and my heart just hurts every time I have to feign that she looks the same as always.

Finding Courage to Cope with the Change

German blood runs deep in my roots, something I've come to appreciate since strength, physical and emotional, is the principle characteristic I've acquired growing up in a family of that ancestry. It's what defines us, what helps us through the tough times and enables us to weather changes in the tide. German fortitude is how my grandmother endured the loss of her husband and the relocation of three of her four children halfway across the country to Texas. German grit is how my family copes with the demise of my grandmother's memory as she slowly slips away from us.

I find my own courage through writing, which has become my saving grace in the face of this debilitating disease. When I write about the time I spent in Delaware as a child, I find my grandmother within the pages. Preserving my memories on paper helps me to process what is occurring and to see Nana Ruth as the woman she truly is. Ironically, one of the greatest sorrows of my life led me to discover one of the greatest joys of my life. Recording recollections of my grandmother before and during her Alzheimer's battle made me realize how much I enjoyed writing about social issues. I have hopes of someday soon writing a novel about the Alzheimer's struggle so that I might help others who are enduring the same trials, cope with the realities of losing a loved one this way. When I write, I am liberated, and strangely enough, documenting my sadness alleviates some of the pain.

Even though writing about this changed version of Nana Ruth can be extremely hard, I owe it to her. For my grandmother is so much more than this moment, or this year, or this disease. There will be a time in the near future when she won't be here physically, even if she is already no longer here mentally. I try to remember this every time we visit her and I feel frustrated that she can't always recall my name. The German strength, her strength, will pull me through and linger long after she has gone. That is her legacy. That is the image I have aspired after since I was a child, and it does not change no matter how weak her mind has become.

So now, whenever I sit on the couch next to Nana Ruth, I stare into those blue eyes I know so well and re-learn the map of her face all over again. In those moments when my grandmother knows my name, she is the one carving a permanent smile on my face so wide I feel as though I could split in half with the joy. When she can't, I swallow the bitter pill of disappointment and know that, for the love of her, I am whoever she wants me to be.

A Fourteen-Year-Old Speaks Out About Frontotemporal Degeneration

Warren P. Russo

Justin Peavey is a teenager, and because his grandmother, great-grandmother, and four great-aunts died of frontotemporal degeneration (FTD), he knows that his mother will probably develop it. He also knows that when they reach middle age, he and his brothers may get it, too. Only 10 percent of FTD cases are the inherited type, but that is the case in his family. Peavey has set out to learn as much as he can about the disease and raise the awareness of others.

Warren P. Russo is a correspondent for the *Daily News* in Newburyport, Massachusetts.

Imagine that you are in perfect health today, but you know that upon reaching middle age, that could begin to change. There are signs that, by the time you reach age 45, a debilitating dementia will begin destroying your brain, taking away your ability to speak and causing you to exhibit increasingly strange behavior—until slowly, your body ceases to function.

SOURCE: Warren P. Russo, "A Crusader for His Cause," *Newburyport News,* April 20, 2012. Copyright © 2012 by The Daily News of Newburyport. All rights reserved. Reproduced by permission.

It's called Frontotemporal Degeneration, or FTD, a degenerative brain disease that attacks the frontal and temporal lobes of the brain, It destroys judgment, personality, speech and mobility. The disease is usually fatal within five to 10 years of a diagnosis. There is no cure for it or preventative treatment. Its progression can also not be slowed once symptoms appear.

Justin Peavey of Merrimac has experience with FTD. He has already lost his grandmother, who died of the disease a few years ago at the age of 67, along with four great-aunts and a great-grandmother, all of whom passed away before their time.

Although only 10 percent of the 50,000 active cases currently identified in the United States are genetic in origin, that is the situation with the maternal side of the Peavey family, which has a lengthy, multi-generational history of the disease. Consequently, Justin now lives with the memories of relatives who died too soon. Now, as a result of genetic testing, he also lives with the knowledge that his mother, Kathy—an intelligent, articulate woman—has tested positive for the gene mutation that causes the disease. Without a medical breakthrough, she has a 95 percent chance of developing dementia while in the prime of her life. Since Kathy has the gene, there is a possibility that Justin and his two brothers also have it. Justin is only 14 years old.

A Crusader for His Cause

Fortunately, this fresh-faced, polite and well-spoken teen is a crusader for his cause, on a mission to raise both money and awareness of FTD in the hope of funding research to find a cure.

An eighth-grade student at Pentucket Middle School, Justin knows as much about the disease as any physician and has developed an effective PowerPoint presentation he shows to anyone who can make a contribution. Although he has raised only $605 so far, he remains un-

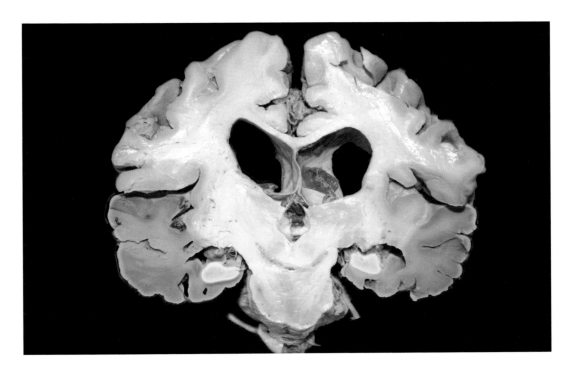

daunted, confident that his fundraising efforts will spark enough interest to somehow make a difference.

While other youngsters his age are playing sports or video games, Justin busies himself meeting with professional fundraisers at Massachusetts General Hospital, where FTD is in the very early stages of research and data gathering.

"They're teaching me how to make better presentations," Justin said, "so that my message will spread awareness of the disease. A group of scientists is looking for a drug discovery and they're finding out more and more about the disease, and the genetic test only came out a few years ago."

Justin remains remarkably positive, a bright student who works as hard at his studies as he does for the disease, and he hopes one day for a dual career—in the performing arts and working with people suffering from dementia.

A frontal view of a brain shows end-stage Alzheimer's with atrophy of the hippocampal formations (in yellow and red), important for memory, with associated enlargement and atrophy of the temporal lobes (in aqua). (© **Living Art Enterprise/Photo Researchers, Inc.**)

An accomplished playwright and author of two e-book short stories with a third one in the works, he is also appearing in his school's production of "Hula Hoops & Halos."

Complicating the research is the duality of the disease, with some cases the result of an inherited genetic mutation, as in Justin's family experience, while the other 90 percent of cases are caused by an unknown factor.

Research is continuing, but without major, sustained funding and enhanced awareness, progress is slow. Kathy Peavey donated her mother's brain and spinal column to the research effort at Mass General.

Since the genetically based variant of FTD is shared within families and affects all of the siblings of anyone who tests positive, her two siblings each have a 50 percent chance of developing dementia from FTD.

"They're still working to find out more about it," Justin said. "It wears away on the brain until it loses its ability to function, but they aren't sure what causes it. They're not sure what the process is yet."

A Son Tells How His Mother Recovered Unexpectedly from Vascular Dementia

Tony Lawrence

Tony Lawrence's mother was an active woman and avid reader even in old age. Then abruptly one day she became incoherent. The doctor who examined her thought she was fine until Lawrence explained that the event she said she was planning had happened many years before. It became evident that she had developed such severe dementia that she could not go on living with the family, so she was moved to a nursing home. The doctors declared that there was no cure. But after about a year had passed, a visiting grand-daughter found that she had suddenly regained her memory. Her mind was just as sharp as it had been before her illness, and she wanted books to read. She remained mentally fine, although too ill physically to leave the nursing home, where she stayed until her death ten years later. No one knew what had caused the temporary dementia; probably it was a small stroke. But, says Lawrence, her experience shows that families should never give up hope.

Lawrence is a self-employed computer consultant.

SOURCE: Tony Lawrence, "Never Give Up Hope With Dementia," http://pcunix.hubpages. com/hub/Never-give-up-hope-with-dementia, July 18, 2011. Copyright © 2011 by A.P. Lawrence. All rights reserved. Reproduced by permission.

My mother was born to fairly well off parents in 1910.

She was a bright child who did well at school and had plans to attend college, but unfortunately those hopes were killed by the stock market crash of 1929.

I don't intend to write a biography of my mother here. I only mention her educational hopes to establish some idea of her interests. She was not what you would call a social person; she loved music and reading but did not seem to have active friendships. I'm not saying that she was unfriendly to people, just that she seemed to desire a more solitary life.

These things are probably completely unimportant for my purposes here.

Let's skip quickly forward. She married and raised a family—my two older sisters and me. She was a devoted parent to her children and grandchildren. She had a good life and my parents lived well.

Late in life, my parents divorced. Again, I feel no need to get into the details of that. After living with my older sister for a bit and then living alone, we built a mother-in-law apartment addition to our home and brought her to live with us. She really couldn't afford to live on her own—it wasn't that she was failing in any way, this was just financially necessary.

I remember asking her if she'd like to do that. I'm not sure she really wanted to, but she knew she was struggling on her own. She accepted quickly.

She had a car, and volunteered at a nearby hospital as a candy-striper. She had a TV and watched Congressional hearings on CSPAN constantly. She had her books and magazines, she had meals with us. She really had no expenses other than her personal needs, so what had been a meager income when she lived alone now became something she barely needed; her bank account grew every month.

Sudden Dementia

She lived with us for a decade. She gave up volunteering and became more sedentary, but her health was good. She kept to herself mostly.

One day I found her babbling. She had closed her door and refused meals for a day or two before that. We assumed she was ill so hadn't been too concerned, but this was very unsettling. We immediately took her to the hospital for evaluation.

Funny story there—the doctor who first examined her came out to see me and told me she was fine and he was ready to discharge her. "In fact", he said, "She told me all about her appointment with her lawyer in Boston tomorrow."

I laughed and explained to him that she hadn't had a lawyer in Boston since the 1950's. I knew exactly what lawyer she meant and even the specific occasion she was remembering—it was when my father started his own business in the '50s. That trip to Boston was to rearrange wills and other documents due to the new business. She was not in the present day.

The doctor went back for another chat and this time came out with a different recommendation. He did say that she was obviously quite brilliant and had him totally fooled until she mentioned a non-existent painting on the wall. He basically explained that there wasn't anything that could be done for her medically. She plainly wouldn't be able to continue living with us, so we found a very nice nursing home nearby and arranged a private room. The money she had saved up for years paid for that for a year or so and then Social Security kicked in after that was all gone. The home kept her in the private room because she was quite anti-social—she did not like anyone there and made that well known.

We visited every week, but it was hard. She didn't know who we were and didn't have much to say to us. We talked to her anyway, but she was mostly disinterested, sometimes very distant and non-responsive. The doctors said this was what we could expect until she died.

I don't remember how long that was. It was more than months, for sure. It may have been a year or more of visiting someone who used to be my mother.

Then one day my daughter went to visit and when she came home I asked her how Gram was as I always did. That had become a perfunctory question by then as there really was never anything to report. She might be more or less cheerful one day or another, but any conversations any of us had were nearly pointless. Still, this was someone we all loved, so we visited and we tried.

My daughter answered "She's fine" and I said something like "Oh, good" and went back to my reading. My daughter became more insistent. "No, Dad, I mean she's *fine*. She knows who I am and she is asking for you!"

I think it took a bit for her to convince me that this was really true. I probably thought that this crafty old woman had fooled my daughter just as she had fooled that doctor. Maybe this was just a new aspect of her personality where she would pretend to know us.

But no, my daughter was not wrong, Apparently my mother had returned to the present world.

So I got in my car and drove over and she really was fine. It was like nothing had ever happened. Bright, alert, looking for something to read—I had to go back home and bring her a pile of books immediately.

Unfortunately her physical health had gone south from sitting all that time, so she could not come back home, but she lived another decade and was very happy until just before her death at 97.

Her Last Years

We had to bring her books every week. Piles of books. One thing about her had changed—she would not watch TV any more. We found out why from the nursing home staff: other residents would wander into her room and sit to watch TV with her. She did not like that; she wanted no friends. We took the TV out.

She had a telephone, but would only use it to call me if she ran out of books or tic-tacs or tissue paper. She had developed a habit of using inordinate amounts of tissue paper—this was the only remaining sign of any remaining mental issues and of course that was minor. Well, a lot of money for tissues, but still very minor.

Most days she was friendly and we'd have good talks. She liked when we brought her old family pictures to look at, but mostly she liked her books. My sister took the brunt of that responsibility, visiting the library every week to bring another large pile to swap out.

She'd sometimes politely ask us to leave within minutes of arrival, saying "You must be so tired! You should go home". That meant she wanted to read. We'd laugh at that—"Gram kicked us out again!"

Other days we had good visits. We'd talk about the books, but toward the very end she stopped doing that. It became obvious that her mind was slipping again because she was only going through the motions of reading. The comprehension was gone. She still knew who we were though, but she was exhibiting difficulties remembering other people we'd mention. When my nephews brought their children to visit, she didn't really know them.

And then she died. Peacefully, in her sleep. I met my sister there that morning and we looked at her frail body in that bed. We were sad, of course, but she was 97 and had not suffered at all. It was good that she could go that way.

Never Give Up

What's the point of all this rather personal stuff?

The point is to never give up. The human brain is an incredible organ. Doctors may say there is no hope and they may very well be right, but they are not always right.

We don't know what caused her mental problem. A little stroke, perhaps, but it doesn't matter. We could have easily abandoned her then—she's "out of it", she doesn't know who we are, there is no point in visiting. Yes, honestly there were times I felt like that.

But she did come back. She rejoined our world. Her mind found its way back to the present time and that gave us the gift of enjoying her last few years.

Don't ever give up.

A Daughter Describes the Problem of Undiagnosed Dementia with Lewy Bodies

Karen Hogan

Karen Hogan's mother suffered from dementia for many years, yet until just before she died, no one knew that it was dementia with Lewy bodies (DLB), an underdiagnosed disease of which few health-care professionals are aware. Because its symptoms overlap with those of Alzheimer's disease and Parkinson's disease, it is hard to recognize; but there are differences, such as the hallucinations that DLB produces. Ten years after the first symptoms appeared, Hogan's mother was both physically and verbally aggressive, paranoid, and unsteady on her feet. She resisted going to a doctor, but finally Hogan got her to a psychiatrist who knew about DLB. Unfortunately, it was too late for the diagnosis to be of much help. Having become violent, she was admitted to a hospital and then a care home, where she died a few weeks later. Hogan believes that earlier treatment could have helped her, or at least made her more comfortable; and she is frustrated by that thought.

Hogan lives in England. She wrote this article for the British newspaper *Daily Mail*.

SOURCE: Karen Hogan, "How Did They Miss the Dementia?" *Mail Online (Daily Mail, London)*, January 14, 2012. Copyright © 2012 by the Daily Mail. All rights reserved. Reproduced by permission.

One of the earliest memories I have of my mother, Mary, is her dancing the Twist to [singer] Chubby Checker at a party during the Sixties. She looked beautiful, with blonde hair cascading down the back of her Dior dress. I was a child, and to me she was a fairytale princess.

Any daughter would cherish this memory, but I hold it close to my heart because for many years before my mother died in 2008, that vivacious woman disappeared.

In the years leading up to her death my mother suffered from dementia with Lewy bodies (DLB), the second most common—yet the most under-diagnosed—form of the disease.

She was one of the many who never received correct treatment for this little understood illness, and as a result her final years were far more uncomfortable than they should have been.

Mum's symptoms started to show many years before she died. Around the age of 65 she complained about losing her purse all the time, but my sister and I thought little of it. She was getting older and, apart from the odd bout of forgetfulness, she was fit, healthy and spritely.

Ten years on, however, she was unrecognisable. She was aggressive—physically and verbally—paranoid and dangerously unsteady on her feet. It was only weeks before she died that it was suggested she might have DLB, by which point it was too late.

It is thought that 150,000 Britons suffer with the condition, although numbers are hard to gauge because it is so difficult to diagnose.

The illness develops when protein deposits called Lewy bodies build up inside the brain, although no one knows why this happens.

This slowly causes the brain to deteriorate in speech and memory, similar to Alzheimer's disease, and movement, as in Parkinson's disease. It is this overlap of symptoms that makes it so hard to identify.

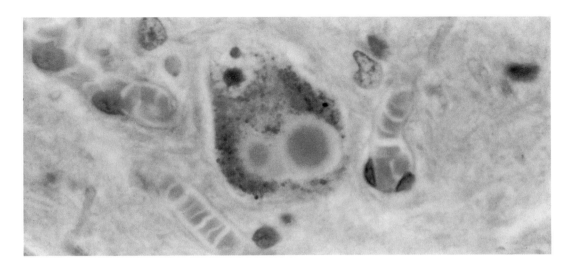

Hallucinations

However, unique to DLB are the hallucinations that develop early. DLB patients also experience moments of lucidity more frequently than with Alzheimer's, even when the disease has progressed. Patients are more prone to falling or fainting from low blood pressure, too.

A micrograph of a human brain shows the Lewy bodies developed in Parkinson's disease. (© Biophoto Associates/ Photo Researchers/Getty Images)

A correct diagnosis is essential. Alzheimer's can be treated with anti-psychotic medication, but DLB sufferers often react badly to these, making the hallucinations more intense. Aricept, another anti-dementia drug, can help, but some DLB patients react badly to it, too.

They can benefit from drugs used to treat the movement problems of Parkinson's—which I am convinced would have helped Mum. But, despite being quite disabled toward the end, she didn't receive these.

DLB patients need careful monitoring because of the changeable nature of the disease.

In 2004, I noticed Mum's gait had become increasingly unsteady so I took her to hospital for tests. The results for Parkinson's came back negative. She had become more aggressive but her memory was still relatively good. I was told she was just becoming wobbly with old age and it was nothing to worry about.

By the following year she was unable to walk unaided and after one nasty accident she was hospitalised with a broken arm. It was during this stay that I saw the extent of her illness. She told me that the doctors and nurses were pumping gas underneath her door to kill her.

I told the doctor about her conspiracy theories and a vague diagnosis of dementia was given. She was discharged two weeks later and given a visiting carer. Few lasted more than a week or two because she was so hostile: she thought they were stealing or plotting to kill her. Later she claimed to see dead dogs in her bed.

I desperately tried to get her to visit a doctor but she refused. She may have been ill, but she was as bloody-minded [contrary] as ever.

Eventually, in 2008 I persuaded her to see a psychiatrist who specialised in geriatric care. His words were a ray of light: everything he saw fitted with DLB and he suggested an appointment at Ealing hospital. I was filled with hope that part of my mother might return, if only a cheeky sparkle in her eye.

But three weeks later she fell again and lost the use of her legs. She was admitted to hospital and started hallucinating. She became increasingly violent so doctors gave her anti-psychotic drugs. Thankfully, she didn't react badly to them but to see her so sedated was heart-breaking. Two weeks later she was transferred to a care home. She was incredibly frail after the fall and two weeks later she passed away.

It was my mother's birthday last week. I always try to remember the good times when I think of her but I can't help but feel frustrated by unanswered questions.

Why could no one see what was wrong sooner? Why aren't healthcare professionals more aware of this debilitating condition?

I hope this article will help raise awareness so that something good comes from my Mum's suffering.

Former President Ronald Reagan Tells the Nation That He Has Alzheimer's Disease

Lou Cannon

Four years after he left office, former president Ronald Reagan became forgetful, which was first noticeable to the public during a short speech he gave during the celebration of his eighty-second birthday. A year and a half later, in 1994, he was diagnosed with Alzheimer's disease. Reagan believed that it was important to increase public understanding of the disease and that publicity surrounding his experience would help to do this, so he wrote a short letter to the American people that has become famous. In it he expressed his feelings about what he knew lay ahead of him, as well as his love for America and his gratitude at having been given the honor of serving as president. This letter was instrumental in raising money for research. After progression of the disease for ten years, Reagan died on June 5, 2004.

Lou Cannon is the author of *President Reagan: The Role of a Lifetime*, a biography of Reagan from which this excerpt is taken.

SOURCE: Lou Cannon, *President Reagan: The Role of a Lifetime*, Public Affairs, 2000. Copyright © 2000 by Perseus Books Group. All rights reserved. Reproduced by permission.

In early 1993, [former president Ronald] Reagan's friends noticed that he seemed increasingly forgetful and tended to repeat himself. The public received its first inkling of his decline on February 6, 1993, when Reagan repeated a toast to Thatcher verbatim during the celebration of his eighty-second birthday at the presidential library. Guests pretended not to notice, but the number of public events on Reagan's schedule were soon reduced. Reagan's last major public appearance was at the funeral of [former president] Richard Nixon on April 27, 1994, where he looked lost. In August 1994, at an annual visit to the Mayo Clinic in Minnesota, Reagan was diagnosed as having the incurable neurological disorder known as Alzheimer's disease. On November 5, Reagan's doctors issued a statement: "Over the past 12 months we began to notice from President Reagan's test results symptoms indicating the possibility of early-stage Alzheimer's disease. Additional testing and an extensive observation over the past few weeks have led us to conclude that President Reagan is entering the early stages of this disease." This candid medical report was overshadowed by Reagan's own description of his plight. In a handwritten letter to the American people dated November 5, 1994, he wrote:

> My Fellow Americans,
>
> I have recently been told that I am one of the millions of Americans who will be afflicted with Alzheimer's Disease.
>
> Upon learning this news, Nancy & I had to decide whether as private citizens we keep this a private matter or whether we would make this news known in a public way.
>
> In the past Nancy suffered from breast cancer and I had my cancer surgeries. We found through our open disclosures we were able to raise public awareness. We were happy that as a result many more people underwent testing. They were treated in early stages and able to return to normal, healthy lives.

So now, we feel it is important to share it with you. In opening our hearts, we hope this might promote greater awareness of this condition. Perhaps it will encourage a clearer understanding of the individuals and families who are affected by it.

At the moment I feel just fine. I intend to live the remainder of the years God gives me on this earth doing the things I have always done. I will continue to share life's journey with my beloved Nancy and my family. I plan to enjoy the great outdoors and stay in touch with my friends and supporters.

Unfortunately, as Alzheimer's Disease progresses, the family often bears a heavy burden. I only wish there was some way I could spare Nancy from this painful experience. When the time comes I am confident that with your help she will face it with faith and courage.

In closing let me thank you, the American people for giving me the great honor of allowing me to serve as your President. When the Lord calls me home, [here Reagan crossed out a word] whenever that may be, I will leave with the greatest love for this country of ours and eternal optimism for its future.

I now begin the journey that will lead me into the sunset of my life. I know that for America there will always be a bright dawn ahead.

Thank you, my friends. May God always bless you.

Sincerely,

Ronald Reagan

Nancy Reagan [the president's wife] called this a "typical Ronnie letter," and she was right. Reagan had a knack for incorporating his experiences into a universal message and explaining large matters in simple ways. His critics complained that he oversimplified, resorting too

Former president
Ronald Reagan and
his wife, Nancy, attend
a holiday event at
the Ronald Reagan
Presidential Library on
November 22, 1994.
It was Reagan's first
public appearance
after revealing his
Alzheimer's diagnosis.
(© AP Images/Mark
J.Terrell)

often to anecdotes, but most of Reagan's stories had a purpose. The principal purpose of his farewell letter is stated clearly in the fourth paragraph, where Reagan said he hoped to promote "greater awareness" of Alzheimer's. No one doubts that such awareness is needed. Four million Americans presently have Alzheimer's. As the elderly population grows, that number is expected to reach fourteen million within fifty years unless a cure is found, according to the Chicago-based Alzheimer's Association. Reagan's letter was a boon to the association and others involved in promoting understanding of the disease and raising money for its cure and treatment.

GLOSSARY

Alzheimer's disease (AD)	The most common cause of dementia in people aged sixty-five and older.
amyloid plaques	Unusual clumps of material found in the tissue between nerve cells. Amyloid plaques, which consist of a protein called beta amyloid along with degenerating bits of neurons and other cells, are a hallmark of Alzheimer's disease.
aphasia	Difficulty finding words and a reduced ability to participate in conversation.
apolipoprotein E (ApoE)	A gene that has been linked to an increased risk of Alzheimer's disease. People with a variant form of the gene, called ApoE epsilon 4, have about ten times the risk of developing Alzheimer's disease.
ataxia	Loss of muscle control.
atherosclerosis	A blood vessel disease characterized by the buildup of fatty substances and other matter in the inner lining of an artery. It can cause vascular dementia if it affects the brain.
beta amyloid	A protein found in the characteristic clumps of tissue (called plaques) that appear in the brains of Alzheimer's patients.
cholinesterase inhibitors	Drugs that slow the breakdown of the neurotransmitter acetylcholine.
cognitive dysfunction	Difficulty with thinking, memory, or concentration.
computed tomography (CAT) scan	A type of brain scan that uses X-rays to detect brain structures.

cortical atrophy	Degeneration of the brain's cortex (outer layer). Cortical atrophy is common in many forms of dementia and may be visible on a brain scan.
cortical dementia	A type of dementia in which the damage primarily occurs in the brain's cortex, or outer layer.
corticobasal degeneration	A progressive disorder characterized by nerve cell loss and atrophy in multiple areas of the brain.
Creutzfeldt-Jakob disease (CJD)	A rare, degenerative, fatal brain disorder believed to be linked to an abnormal form of a protein called a prion.
dementia	A term for a collection of symptoms that significantly impair thinking, normal activities, and relationships. Many diseases can produce dementia.
dementia pugilistica	A form of dementia caused by head trauma such as that experienced by boxers. It is also called chronic traumatic encephalopathy or boxer's syndrome.
electroencephalogram (EEG)	A medical procedure that records patterns of electrical activity in the brain.
frontotemporal dementias (FTD)	A group of dementias characterized by degeneration of nerve cells, especially those in the frontal and temporal lobes of the brain.
HIV-associated dementia	A dementia that results from infection with the human immunodeficiency virus (HIV) that causes AIDS. It can cause widespread destruction of the brain's white matter.
Huntington's disease	A degenerative hereditary disorder caused by a faulty gene for a protein called huntington. The disease causes degeneration in many regions of the brain and spinal cord, and patients eventually develop severe dementia.
Lewy body dementia (LBD) or dementia with Lewy bodies (DLB)	One of the most common types of progressive dementia, characterized by the presence of abnormal structures called Lewy bodies in the brain.

magnetic resonance imaging (MRI)	A diagnostic imaging technique that uses magnetic fields and radio waves to produce detailed images of body structures.
mild cognitive impairment (MCI)	A condition associated with impairments in understanding and memory not severe enough to be diagnosed as dementia, but more pronounced than those associated with normal aging.
multi-infarct dementia	A type of vascular dementia caused by numerous small strokes in the brain.
myelin	A fatty substance that coats and insulates nerve cells.
neurodegeneration	The breaking down of tissue in the nervous system, resulting in the dysfunction or death of neurons.
neurofibrillary tangles	Bundles of twisted filaments within neurons, a characteristic feature found in the brains of Alzheimer's patients. These tangles are largely made up of a protein called tau.
neuron	A nerve cell.
neurotransmitter	A type of chemical such as acetylcholine that transmits signals from one neuron to another.
Parkinson's dementia	A secondary dementia that sometimes occurs in people with advanced Parkinson's disease, which is primarily a movement disorder. Many Parkinson's patients have the characteristic amyloid plaques and neurofibrillary tangles found in Alzheimer's disease, but it is not yet clear if the diseases are linked.
Pick's disease	A type of frontotemporal dementia in which certain nerve cells become abnormal and swollen before they die. The brains of people with Pick's disease have abnormal structures, called Pick bodies, inside the neurons.
plaques	Unusual clumps of material found in the tissues of the brain in Alzheimer's disease. *See also* amyloid plaques.
post-traumatic dementia	A dementia brought on by a single traumatic brain injury. It is much like dementia pugilistica, but usually also includes long-term memory problems.

primary dementia	Dementia, such as Alzheimer's disease, that is not the result of another disease.
primary progressive aphasia	A type of frontotemporal dementia resulting in deficits in language functions. Many, but not all, people with this type of aphasia eventually develop symptoms of dementia.
progressive dementia	Dementia that gets worse over time, gradually interfering with more and more cognitive abilities.
protein	A biochemical compound that facilitates a biological function.
secondary dementia	Dementia that occurs as a consequence of another disease or an injury.
senile dementia	An outdated term that reflects the formerly widespread belief that dementia was a normal part of aging. The word *senile* is derived from a Latin term that roughly means "old age."
subcortical dementia	Dementia that affects parts of the brain below the outer brain layer, or cortex.
substance-induced persisting dementia	Dementia caused by abuse of substances such as alcohol and recreational drugs that persists even after the substance abuse has ended.
tau protein	A protein that helps the functioning of microtubules, which are part of the cell's structural support and help to deliver substances throughout the cell. In Alzheimer's disease, tau is changed in a way that causes it to twist into pairs of helical filaments that collect into tangles.
TIA (transitory ischemic attack)	A mini stroke lasting only a few minutes.
transmissible spongiform encephalopathies	Part of a family of human and animal diseases in which the brain becomes filled with holes resembling a sponge when examined under a microscope. CJD is the most common of the known transmissible spongiform encephalopathies.
vascular dementia	Dementia caused by impaired blood circulation to the brain, usually due to strokes or repeated TIAs.

CHRONOLOGY

1817   James Parkinson, an English scientist, describes the disease now known by his name.

1872   George Huntington, an American physician, describes Huntington's disease.

1876   Jean-Martin Charcot names Parkinson's disease.

1892   Arnold Pick, a Czech neurologist, describes Pick's disease, a form of frontotemporal degeneration (FTD).

1906   Alois Alzheimer, a German psychiatrist, describes the amyloid plaques found in the brains of people with the neurodegenerative disease that comes to bear his name.

1910   Emil Kraepelin, a German psychiatrist, names Alzheimer's disease.

1912   Friedrich Lewy, a German American neurologist, describes the abnormal protein deposits in the brain now known as Lewy bodies.

1921   Otto Loewi, an Austrian pharmacologist, discovers neurotransmitters.

1957   The National Parkinson Foundation is incorporated.

1958   Arvid Carlsson, a Swedish scientist, finds dopamine to
         be a transmitter in the brain and proposes that it has a
         role in Parkinson's disease.

1966   The first academic Department of Neurobiology is es-
         tablished at Harvard University.

1967   Famous poet and songwriter Woody Guthrie dies of
         Huntington's disease, and his wife creates the organiza-
         tion that later becomes the Huntington's Disease Soci-
         ety of America.

1968   The first study reporting improvements in patients with
         Parkinson's disease resulting from treatment with L-
         dopa is published.

1977   Scientists conclude that the symptoms of dementia
         occurring before age sixty-five, to which the term
         "Alzheimer's disease" was then confined, are the same
         as those of what was previously called "senile demen-
         tia" and believed to be due simply to aging. Not until
         later was the term "senile dementia" officially dropped,
         however.

1979   The Alzheimer's Association is founded.

1981   Magnetic resonance imaging is first used to record ab-
         normalities in the brain and along the spinal cord.

1984   The first clinical guidelines for diagnosing Alzheimer's
         disease are published.

1993   The gene responsible for Huntington's disease is
         identified.

1994   Former president Ronald Reagan writes a letter to the American people stating that he has Alzheimer's disease. This results in greater awareness of the disease and increased support for research into its causes.

1995   An international consortium of researchers establishes guidelines for diagnosis of dementia with Lewy bodies and decides on that as the official name for it.

1996   Aricept, the first drug for Alzheimer's disease, is approved.

2011   The National Institute on Aging/Alzheimer's Association Diagnostic Guidelines for Alzheimer's Disease is published, marking a major change in how experts think about and study the disease.

2011   Congress passes the National Alzheimer's Project Act, which will create a national strategic plan to address and overcome the rapidly escalating crisis of Alzheimer's disease.

2012   The World Health Organization issues a major report on the growing problem throughout the world of dementia caused by neurodegenerative disorders.

ORGANIZATIONS TO CONTACT

The editors have compiled the following list of organizations concerned with the issues debated in this book. The descriptions are derived from materials provided by the organizations. All have publications or information available for interested readers. The list was compiled on the date of publication of the present volume; the information provided here may change. Be aware that many organizations take several weeks or longer to respond to inquiries, so allow as much time as possible.

Alzheimer's Association
225 N. Michigan Ave.,
Fl. 17,
Chicago, IL 60601
(800) 272-3900
website: www.alz.org

The Alzheimer's Association works on a global, national, and local level to enhance care and support for all those affected by Alzheimer's and related dementias. It is the largest private nonprofit funder of Alzheimer's research. Its website contains extensive information on all aspects of dementia for patients, caregivers, and the public, including publications that can be downloaded. It also offers a section for teens that includes videos.

Alzheimer's Foundation of America (AFA)
322 Eighth Ave.,
7th Fl.,
New York, NY 10001
e-mail: info@alzfdn.org
website: www.alzfdn.org
(866) 232-8484
fax: (646) 638-1546

The AFA unites more than sixteen hundred member organizations that are dedicated to meeting the educational, social, emotional, and practical needs of individuals with Alzheimer's disease and related illnesses, as well as those of their caregivers and families. Its branch for teens, www.afateens.org, seeks to mobilize teenagers nationwide to raise awareness of Alzheimer's disease, as well as to educate and support teens whose family members are affected by the disease.

Association for Frontotemporal Degeneration (AFTD)
Radnor Station
Bldg. #2, Ste. 320,
290 King of Prussia Rd.,
Radnor, PA 19087
(267) 514-7221
e-mail: info@theaftd
.org
website: www.theaftd
.org

The AFTD is a nonprofit organization whose mission is to promote and fund research into frontotemporal degeneration (FTD); provide information, education, and support to persons diagnosed with an FTD disorder as well as to their families and caregivers; and bring about greater public awareness of the nature and prevalence of FTD. Its website contains information about the disorder and current research related to it.

Family Caregiver Alliance (FCA)
785 Market St.,
Ste. 750,
San Francisco, CA
94103
(800) 445-8106
fax: (415) 434-3508
website: www.care
giver.org

The FCA is a community-based nonprofit organization addressing the needs of families and friends providing long-term care at home. It offers programs at national, state, and local levels to support and sustain caregivers, serve as a public voice for them, and champion their cause through education, services, research, and advocacy. Its website contains a large amount of material useful to caregivers, as well as information about research and public policy related to caregiving.

Huntington's Disease Society of America (HDSA)
8303 Arlington Blvd.,
Ste. 210,
Fairfax, VA 22031
(703) 204-4634
fax: (703) 573-3047
website: www.hdsa.org

The HDSA is a national nonprofit health organization dedicated to improving the lives of people with Huntington's disease and their families. Its goals are to promote and support research and medical efforts to eradicate Huntington's disease, assist people and families affected by Huntington's disease to cope with the problems presented by the disease, and educate the public and health professionals about Huntington's disease. It is composed of regional chapters, each of which has its own section of the national website.

Lewy Body Dementia Association (LBDA)
912 Killian Hill Rd. SW, Lilburn, GA 30047
(800) 539-9767
fax: (480) 422-5434
e-mail: lbda@lbda.org
website: www.lbda.org

The LBDA is a nonprofit organization dedicated to raising awareness of the Lewy body dementias (LBD), supporting patients, their families and caregivers, and promoting scientific advances. Its website contains information about LBD, including reports, an archived newsletter, and other materials that can be downloaded, as well as resources for caregivers and a discussion forum.

National Institute of Neurological Disorders and Stroke (NINDS)
NIH Neurological Institute, PO Box 5801, Bethesda, MD 20824
(800) 352-9424
website: www.ninds.nih .gov

The NINDS is part of the National Institutes of Health, an agency of the US Department of Health and Human Services. It conducts, fosters, coordinates, and guides research on the causes, prevention, diagnosis, and treatment of neurological disorders and stroke and collects and disseminates research information. Its website contains detailed, specific information about all neurological disorders, including dementia.

National Institute on Aging (NIA)
31 Center Dr., MSC 2292, Bethesda, MD 20892
(800) 222-2225
e-mail: niaic@nia.nih .gov
website: www.nia.nih .gov

The NIA is part of the National Institutes of Health, an agency of the US Department of Health and Human Services. Its mission is to discover what may contribute to a healthy old age as well as to understand and address the disease and disability sometimes associated with growing older. Its research program covers a broad range of areas, from the study of basic cellular changes that occur with age to the examination of the biomedical, social, and behavioral aspects of age-related conditions, including Alzheimer's disease.

National Parkinson Foundation (NPF)
1501 NW Ninth Ave./
Bob Hope Rd., Miami,
FL 33136-1494
(800) 327-4545
fax: (305) 243-6073
e-mail: contact@parkin
son.org
website: www.parkin
son.org

The NPF is a nonprofit organization focused on meeting needs in the care and treatment of people with Parkinson's disease. Its mission is to improve the quality of care through research, education, and outreach. Its website contains detailed information about the disease and the problems encountered by people who have it, plus many personal stories.

Parkinson's Disease Foundation (PDF)
1359 Broadway,
Ste. 1509, New York,
NY 10018
(212) 923-4700
fax: (212) 923-4778
website: www.pdf.org

The PDF is a nonprofit organization that is a leading national presence in Parkinson's disease research, education, and public advocacy. It funds promising scientific research while supporting people living with Parkinson's through educational programs and services. Its website includes downloadable archives of print newsletters, e-newsletters, and brochures as well as general information about the disease. It also offers online educational seminars.

University of California Institute for Memory Impairments and Neurological Disorders (UCI MIND)
2642 Biological
Sciences III, Irvine, CA
92697-4545
(949) 824-3253
fax: (949) 824-0885
website: www.alz.uci
.edu

UCI MIND seeks to conduct research to enhance the quality of life for the elderly by identifying factors and lifestyle approaches that promote successful brain aging. Among its activities is the training and education of graduate students and postdoctoral fellows in the field of brain aging and neurodegeneration. Its website contains information about the neurodegenerative disorders that most commonly affect older people.

FOR FURTHER READING

Books

Marjorie N. Allen, Susan Dublin, and P.J. Kimmerly, *A Look Inside Alzheimer's*. New York: Demos Health, 2012.

Virginia Bell and David Troxel, *A Dignified Life: The Best Friends Approach to Alzheimer's Care—A Guide for Family Caregivers*. Deerfield Beach, FL: HCI, 2012.

Cathie Borrie, *The Long Hello: The Other Side of Alzheimer's*. Vancouver, BC: Nightwing, 2010.

Pauline Boss, *Loving Someone Who Has Dementia: How to Find Hope While Coping with Stress and Grief*. San Francisco: Jossey-Bass, 2011.

Dwayne J. Clark, *My Mother, My Son: A True Story of Love, Determination, and Memories Lost*. Redmond, WA: Aegis Living, 2012.

Tam Cummings, *Untangling Dementia: A Guide to Understanding Alzheimer's and Other Dementias*. Largo, FL: Global Geriatrics, 2012.

P. Murali Doraiswamy and Lisa P. Gwyther, *The Alzheimer's Action Plan*. New York: St, Martin's, 2008.

Thomas Graboys, *Life in the Balance: A Physician's Memoir of Life, Love, and Loss with Parkinson's Disease and Dementia*. New York: Union Square, 2008.

Richard S. Isaacson, *Alzheimer's Treatment, Alzheimer's Prevention: A Patient and Family Guide*. Miami Beach, FL: AD Education Consultants, 2012.

Judith London, *Connecting the Dots: Breakthroughs in Communication as Alzheimer's Advances*. Oakland, CA: New Harbinger, 2009.

Nancy L. Mace and Peter V. Rabins, *The 36-Hour Day: A Family Guide to Caring for People Who Have Alzheimer Disease, Related Dementias, and Memory Loss*. Baltimore: Johns Hopkins, 2011.

Nancy Pearce, *Inside Alzheimer's.* Taylors, SC: Forrason, 2011.

Barry Petersen, *Jan's Story: Love Lost to the Long Goodbye of Alzhemier's.* Lake Forest, CA: Behler, 2010.

Lisa Radin and Gary Radin, *What If It's Not Alzheimer's? A Caregiver's Guide to Dementia.* Amherst, NY: Prometheus, 2008.

Nataly Rubinstein, *Alzheimer's Disease and Other Dementias— the Caregiver's Complete Survival Guide.* Minneapolis: Two Harbors, 2011.

Robert B. Santulli, *The Alzheimer's Family: Helping Caregivers Cope.* New York: Norton, 2011.

Maria Shriver, *Alzheimer's in America: The Shriver Report on Women and Alzheimer's.* New York: Free Press, 2011.

Helen Buell Whitworth and Jim Whitworth, *A Caregiver's Guide to Lewy Body Dementia.* New York: Demos Health, 2010.

Periodicals and Internet Sources

Pam Belluck, "New Drug Trial Seeks to Stop Alzheimer's Before It Starts," *New York Times*, May 15, 2012.

Sandra Blakeslee, "A Disease That Allowed Torrents of Creativity," *New York Times*, April 8, 2008.

Jane E. Brody, "When Lapses Are Not Just Signs of Aging," *New York Times*, September 5, 2011.

Katy Butler, "What Broke My Father's Heart," *New York Times Magazine*, June 18, 2010.

Daniel J. DeNoon, "Descent into Alzheimer's: Detailed Alzheimer's Timeline Starts 25 Years Before Severe Dementia," WebMD, July 11, 2012. www.webmd.com/alzheimers/news/20120711/descent- into-alzheimers-detailed.

Kerry Hannon, "Love You, Dad. Alzheimer's Care and My Family's Story," *Forbes*, June 17, 2012. www.forbes.com/sites/kerryhannon/2012/06/17/love-you-dad-alzheimers-care-and-my-familys-story.

Gina Kolata, "In Preventing Alzheimer's, Mutation May Aid Drug Quest," *New York Times*, July 11, 2012.

Kay Lazar and Matt Carroll, "A Rampant Prescription, a Hidden Peril," *Boston Globe*, April 29, 2012. http://articles.boston.com/2012-04-29/news/31478153_l_nursing-home-antipsychotics-skilled- nursing-center.

Angela Lunde, "Myths, Misconceptions Interfere with Alzheimer's Diagnosis, Care," Mayo Clinic, June 26, 2012. www.mayo clinic.com/health/alzheimers-stigma/MY02148.

Marilynn Marchione, "Last Drugs Standing: Key Alzheimer Results Coming," Boston.com, July 13, 2012. www.boston.com /2012/07/13/entry-cont/o7mFixDleEN5A9fdwfuLKL/single page.html.

Marie Marley, "Alzheimer's and the Devil Called Denial," *Huffington Post*, June 20, 2012. www.huffingtonpost.com/marie -marley/alzheimers_b_1609207.html.

Rosie Mestel, "Alzheimer's, Parkinson's, More—Due to Infectious Proteins?," *Los Angeles Times*, June 29, 2012. http://articles.latimes .com/2012/jun/29/news/la-heb-alzheimers-parkinsons-infectious -proteins-20120622.

National Institutes of Health, "NIH Consensus Development Conference Statement on Preventing Alzheimer's Disease and Cognitive Decline," April 28, 2010. http://consensus.nih .gov/2010/docs /alz/ALZ_Final_Statement.pdf.

Catharine Paddock, "Stress as Risk Factor for Alzheimer's Under Investigation," *Medical News Today*, June 26, 2012. www .medicalnewstoday.com/articles/247092.php.

Alice Park, "Is Alzheimer's Caused by Contagious Proteins?," *Time*, February 3, 2012.

Alice Park, "Scientists Identify Rare Gene Mutation That Protects Against Alzheimer's," *Time*, July 12, 2012. http://health land.time.com/2012/07/12/scientists-identify-rare-gene -mutation-that-protects- against-alzheimers.

Laura Sanders, "Like a Prion, Alzheimer's Protein Seeds Itself in the Brain," *Science News*, July 14, 2012. www.sciencenews.org /view/generic/id/341619/title/Like_a_prion_Alzheimers_pro tein_seeds_itself_in_the_brain.

ScienceDaily, "Alzheimer's Plaques in PET Brain Scans Identify Future Cognitive Decline," July 11, 2012. www.sciencedaily.com /releases/2012/07/120711210100.htm.

ScienceDaily, "Low Education Level Linked to Alzheimer's, Study Shows," October 1, 2007. www.sciencedaily.com/releases /2007/10/071001172855.htm.

ScienceDaily, "Timeline Maps Brain's Descent into Alzheimer's," July 11, 2012. www.sciencedaily.com/releases/2012/07/120711 205859.htm.

ScienceDaily, "Why More Education Lowers Dementia Risk," July 25, 2010. www.sciencedaily.com/releases/2010/07/100725 203914.htm.

Thadd Scott. "Study: A Timetable for Alzheimer's Disease Has Been Discovered," Examiner.com, July 14, 2012. www.exam iner.com/article/study-a-timetable-for-alzheimer-s-disease -has-been-discovered.

Tiffany Sharples, "Can Language Skills Ward Off Alzheimer's? A Nuns' Study," *Time*, July 9, 2009. www.time.com/time/health /article/0,8599,1909420,00.html#ixzzlsl7F8sXO.

Christopher Tokin, "New Drugs Aimed at Ending Alzheimer's Decline," ABC News, July 13, 2012. http://abcnews.go.com /Health/Alzheimers/drugs-aimed-ending-alzheimers-decline /story?id=16766730#.UAIAFZH8JK0.

Michael Waldhotz, "Alzheimer's Drug Research at Make or Break Juncture," *Forbes*, July 13, 2012. www.forbes.com/sites /michaelwaldholz/2012/07/13/alzheimers-drug-research-at -make-or-break-juncture.

Alice G. Walton, "An Alzheimer's Researcher Ends Up on the Drug She Helped Invent," *Atlantic*, June 19, 2012. www.the atlantic.com/health/archive/2012/06/an-alzheimers- researcher -ends-up-on-the-drug-she-helped-invent/258229.

INDEX